GREAT
AMERICAN
Conservative
WOMEN

GREAT AMERICAN *Conservative* WOMEN

A COLLECTION OF SPEECHES
FROM THE CLARE BOOTHE LUCE
POLICY INSTITUTE

DEDICATION

THIS BOOK IS DEDICATED to the countless students who face—and challenge—radical liberal orthodoxy every day.

THANKS

WITHOUT THE THOUSANDS OF CONTRIBUTORS and friends of the Clare Boothe Luce Policy Institute who regularly send donations to support us, there would not have been a volume titled *Great American Conservative Women*.

Special thanks for the completion of this project go to all of the staff at the Clare Boothe Luce Policy Institute: Mychele Brickner, program officer, who took the lead on this book project and carried it start to finish; Lisa De Pasquale, program director, who does all the invitation, setup work, and transcribing of speeches for the monthly Conservative Women's Network lunches where these speeches were given; Jeanne O'Connor, administrative director, who helps with the administration of all our programs; and Lil Tuttle whose editing and advice are invaluable. And without Trish Bozell's outstanding editing, this book could never have made it to press.

I am especially grateful to Becky Norton Dunlop and Bridgett Wagner at The Heritage Foundation who make putting on the monthly Conservative Women's Network lunches with them such a pleasure.

I also thank my husband Ron and my sons RJ, Danny, and Thomas for their unfailing love and support in all my undertakings. ∎

Michelle Easton
Clare Boothe Luce Policy Institute

Published by

THE CLARE BOOTHE LUCE POLICY INSTITUTE

112 Elden Street, Suite P

Herndon, VA 20170

1-888-891-4288

www.cblpolicyinstitute.org

Edited by Patricia B. Bozell.

Cover design and graphic layout by Marja Walker.

Front cover photographs are of speakers whose speeches are included in this book. From left to right they are: Michelle Easton, Dr. Laura Schlessinger, Ann Coulter, Star Parker, Linda Chavez, Phyllis Schlafly (top right), and Dr. Jeane Kirkpatrick (lower right).

FIRST EDITION

CONTENTS

INTRODUCTION

NOT LONG AGO, A SUMMER INTERN at the Clare Boothe Luce Policy Institute asked her Rutgers University professor if she could write a thesis on conservative women leaders. She received the short answer: "There are no conservative women leaders."

This astonishing message—if you want to be a successful woman you can't be a conservative—is pounded into young women across the nation by liberal feminists and their acolytes.

This book explodes such liberal arrogance. *Great American Conservative Women* bulges with the lives, accomplishments, and views of outstanding women leaders. They represent all walks of life—from a star of Broadway to an ambassador to the United Nations, from an internationally syndicated talk show host and a nationally syndicated columnist to political leaders, editors, authors, public policy leaders, family and child advocates, CEOs, and mothers.

Unlike liberals, conservatives have never thought of their major female figures as some form of minority. Clare Boothe Luce, Jeane Kirkpatrick, and Dr. Laura Schlessinger are simply great leaders. At the Clare Boothe Luce Policy Institute (sponsors of these talks, along with The Heritage Foundation), we believe that our failure to appreciate these, among other prominent women, allows the Left a free field to highlight only feminist icons.

Why did the Clare Boothe Luce Policy Institute feel the need to publish this book? Why aren't these women already held up as role models in our schools, colleges, and in the media?

Thirty or so years ago, the women who called themselves feminists were taking off their underclothes and burning them in public places as a statement of their liberation. Most people snickered at these bra burners and went on to attend to serious matters.

But today, these same women are running the universities and overseeing Women's Studies programs, courses, and institutes, with the media's hearty blessing. They shrug off the incredible accomplishments of women like those we feature while promoting narrow-minded leftists who scorn people of faith and traditional families. They disdain conservative women leaders because, by their definition, conservative women can't be leaders.

These former bra burners, with their leftist programs and rigid ideology, are not interested in producing successful women; they want to produce little liberals, marching behind in unquestioning left-wing obedience. Any deviation from their orthodoxy and you become a non-person, not worthy of inclusion in Women's Studies or other leftist courses. In a classic illustration, when Texas conservative Kay Bailey Hutchison ran for the U.S. Senate, Gloria Steinem, grand mistress of the feminist movement, called her a "female impersonator," and explained that someone "who looks like us but thinks like them is worse than having no one at all"—i.e., a non-person.

The Clare Boothe Luce Policy Institute was founded in 1993 to train young women to be strong and articulate leaders for the future. We hold up America's outstanding women as role models and offer them alternatives to the sort of dogmatic thinking shown above. We offer an intern program, conduct research, sponsor conferences, seminars, lunches, and many other events. We promote outstanding conservative women and their ideas.

A few years later, in 1999, the Clare Boothe Luce Policy Institute and The Heritage Foundation joined to sponsor monthly Conservative Women's Network (CWN) luncheons featuring outstanding women leaders. A number of these are covered by C-SPAN, which takes the message of these outstanding leaders into 70 million homes. The response has been so overwhelming that, aside from the reason stated above, we decided to select a sampling of these speeches and present them to you in book form. The result is *Great American Conservative Women*. The speakers provide conservative solutions to the challenges of our time, refuting the liberal message. They beg to disagree and voice their opinions with force and a heavy dose of humor.

Many of the young women we work with at the Clare Boothe Luce Policy Institute face derision when they voice an opinion contrary to the established liberal dogma. Doing so at the university level is to risk being battered intellectually, by teachers and fellow students alike. "I didn't expect to be ridiculed and bullied every time I expressed an opinion contrary to the teacher's, or ostracized by my fellow students," another of our brave interns wrote. This kind of treatment caught the attention of Ann Coulter, an attorney who specializes in constitutional law, acts on her beliefs, and is, incidentally, our most popular campus lecturer. She explains in these pages: "I love to speak on college campuses. The environments are so hegemonically left-wing that students who bring me to speak are invariably the rebels. They're always bright, politically active, and appear to wake up every morning thinking: What can I do today to annoy liberals? Apparently, bringing me to speak is one of the popular options."

Then there are the male-haters, preferably white adult males, but boys will do. It's hard to decide whether malevolence or lack of humor predominates; as, for example:

"At Brown University, makeshift graveyards were created on the sports field, with each headstone declaring a statistic about men's violence against women," writes yet another intern. This childish display is given short shrift by syndicated columnist and author Suzanne Fields, who says in her talk, "The changing culture and feminism loosened the traditional demands on men as it freed choices for women...Women who wanted the pleasure of sexuality without commitment got what they asked for."

Christina Hoff Sommers, prolific author and another of our popular campus lecturers, points out that today little boys are routinely punished for acting like little boys in order to strip them of their masculinity and make them androgynous creatures. In a recent egregious incident, four little boys were suspended for three days from their kindergarten for using their fingers as guns in a game of cops and robbers!

But it won't work. Little boys will continue to act like little boys. It is their nature. Sommers says in her talk, "Hasbro Toys...tested a playhouse the company was considering marketing to both boys and girls. But it soon emerged that girls and boys did not interact with the playhouse structure in the same way. The girls dressed the dolls, kissed them, and played house. The boys catapulted the baby carriage from the roof. A Hasbro general manager came up with an explanation: boys and girls are different."

And, of course, beware the hard-core feminism. In another snippet from a Luce Policy Institute intern:

"At Berkeley, well-know porn star Nina Hartley was asked to speak to the campus in honor of 'women's empowerment' and discuss how she took her sexuality into her own hands and learned to 'experiment' with bisexuality, sex toys, and came to participate in over 550 pornographic films. Held up as a role model for women, Hartley, a self-proclaimed feminist, declared that students who need a study break should engage in sexual activity with one another for experimentation value." Higher education at the feminist best. Clearly there is a need for appropriate role models for young women.

This perverted feminism is a far cry from the honest fight for equality that fired the old women's movement. "The once valiant women's movement that I embraced," says Dr. Laura

Schlessinger, internationally syndicated talk show personage, "is no longer about fairness, equality, opportunity, and respect for *all* women—it's about the politics of selective diversity and, ultimately, of divisiveness. It is anti-female, anti-family, and anti-children."

What might astonish readers of *Great American Conservative Women* is that most of these eminent women regard their families as the most important element of their lives. Some speak eloquently about their roles as wives and mothers.

Ambassador to the United Nations Jeane Kirkpatrick tells us: "People have often said to me, what did I do that was the most interesting thing in my life. The answer is having a baby...Having and raising babies is more interesting than making speeches at the United Nations. Believe me."

Clare Boothe Luce, relates Letitia Baldrige, her assistant while Luce was ambassador to Rome, "had dropped leaflets from a biplane for women's right to vote and done other things to help women, yet she was steadfastly against abortion"—as were the original suffragettes Elizabeth Cady Stanton and Susan B. Anthony.

Kate Griffin, stay-at-home mother, freelance writer, and speaker puts it poignantly: "There is a powerful social stigma, thanks to the resounding success of the radical feminist movement, to being a stay-at-home mother...At a recent cocktail party someone said that I must have a real need to be considered important and useful. But I am."

Karlyn Bowman, a highly regarded researcher and poll reader, puts it succinctly by citing a recent survey, which points out that women, despite continual battering by the feminists, cling to the ideal of marriage and family: "Most young women today say that they want to marry and have families...their ideal."

We conservative women are not stiff with self-importance; we understand the irony of life, and we have the humility to see the world—its goods and its faults—and ourselves, with good will, open minds, and laughter. (Dr. Kirkpatrick relates an experience in the Situation Room—incidentally, the first woman ever to have entered the National Security Planning Group, the NSPG, that holy of holies in the basement of the White House—and of the sudden appearance of...a mouse. This intrepid adventurer had somehow made its way through locked doors, evading alarms and a contingent of Marines with guns at the ready. "Well, we looked at the mouse, the mouse looked at us, and the mouse walked across the room and disappeared.")

We also believe in good and evil, truth and lies. The distinction between them is often obscured by liberal incoherency. Randall Phillips, child star of the hit musical *Annie*, says simply: "We have the message of truth." Other examples:

■ "Without the ability to own private property, there is no freedom" (Helen Chenoweth-Hage, U.S. House of Representatives, 1994-2000).

■ "Do you realize that the laws in our country exact a more severe punishment for destroying condor eggs than for destroying another human being?" (Becky Norton Dunlop, former cabinet member of Governor George Allen of Virginia).

■ "The federal government now owns more than a third of all the land in the United States" (Virginia Thomas, former top aide to House Majority Leader Richard Armey).

■ "Medicare regulations consist of 134,000 pages" (Virginia Thomas).

■ "You cannot understand morality without God. Today we could have 270 million people out there determining for themselves what right and wrong is—like that young man did in San Diego who fired on his classmates. He didn't think he did anything wrong" (Star Parker, former single welfare mother, founder and president of Coalition on Urban Renewal and Education).

Every week I receive calls from students and others asking for a book that highlights America's outstanding conservative women—and here it is!

Read on and find out about women who are not chained to liberal ideology, whatever its manifestation—whether feminism, environmentalism, multiculturalism, diversity, or secularism—but think for themselves. Read on and breathe the clean air of womanhood at its best: mature, accomplished, nurturing, intelligent, and God-fearing. ■

—Michelle Easton
Founder and President
Clare Boothe Luce Policy Institute

THE THIRD DAY I WAS THERE, I HEARD SHRIEKS, YELLING, AND POUNDING DOWN BELOW. I RUSHED DOWN TO THE KITCHEN AND I FOUND THE CHEF AND THE MAITRE D'HO-TEL GOING AT EACH OTHER WITH KITCHEN KNIVES. THAT'S WHEN I REALIZED I WAS IN FOR A REAL RIDE WITH THIS JOB.

—LETITIA BALDRIGE

I Worked for the Real Clare Boothe Luce

BY LETITIA BALDRIGE
WASHINGTON, D.C., DECEMBER 8, 2000
EXCERPTS FROM A SPEECH AT THE CONSERVATIVE WOMEN'S NETWORK

WHEN CLARE LUCE WAS APPOINTED ambassador to Rome in 1953 I was asked to join her staff in Rome. I was terrified. It seemed that everyone I knew said awful things about her and now prophesied, "Oh, you'll come home in two weeks."

They couldn't have been more wrong. The constant criticism from both men and women stemmed, I think, from jealousy.

LETITIA BALDRIGE has authored eighteen books on manners and entertaining. Her latest is an autobiography, *A Lady, First*. She is the president of Letitia Baldrige Enterprises, a company specializing in management training. She spent many years as the special assistant to Ambassador Clare Boothe Luce at the Villa Taverna in Rome. She lives in Washington, D.C., with her husband, Robert Hollensteiner.

PHOTO: Letitia Baldrige (center) with Michelle Easton (left) (Clare Boothe Luce Policy Institute), and Bridgett Wagner (right) (The Heritage Foundation), alongside portrait of Clare Boothe Luce.

Anyway, I went over there, sight unseen, to be social secretary, and, as it turned out, her aide at the American Embassy residence, the Villa Taverna. It was a beautiful sixteenth-century villa with lovely gardens and its own entries to the catacombs.

We used to have dinner parties out of doors on travertine marble tables with benches. The terrace was lit by iron pots of burning oil on the ancient fragments of walls and columns. The ilex trees that crossed over the dining terrace were illuminated and formed a canopy. The only other light came from the hurricane lamps on the tables. It was like being in a special movie set, it was so beautiful and romantic.

I arrived at the Villa Taverna, as I said before, just terrified. I had on my three-inch high heels, so I stood six-four. I walked into her bedroom, where I had been told to meet her. She always worked in bed. She was in a pale blue dressing gown—she had been working all day—wearing her bedroom slippers. And she looked up at this overwhelmingly tall young woman and said, "My God, do you type, too?"

I said, "Yes, I do, very well." I proved not to be that good a stenographer, which was okay because my job was running the residence, entertaining, and handling all of the telephone calls that came in and went out, most of them in Italian. Trouble is I had lied on my resumé and said I was completely fluent in Italian.

I realized I had exactly two weeks to get it down pat. I had taken Italian lessons in Washington given by Signora Sera of the Italian Embassy who used to invite me over for Sunday lunch. She assembled all of her large Italian family and made this elaborate Italian meal. As we talked, I learned all the ways to pronounce the *primi piatti* and kitchen words, but I didn't know a thing about diplomatic language, only culinary.

Suddenly, here was this stream of Italian coming at me on the telephone, and I realized I was going to lose my job if I didn't act fast—so I did. I would tell the Italian caller, "Per favore, *lentamente*, per favore." (Slowly, please.) And they kindly slowed down, so I could hear each syllable. They'd answer, "Voglio parlare con..." (slowly enunciated).

It's amazing how people will help you out. So in two weeks, I knew I would keep my job. The Luces spoke no Italian, so they couldn't check up on me!

I took care of the ambassador's personal mail and learned how to write in her style. She liked my enthusiasm in my letters for her signature, but she calmed down some of my gushiness while teaching me how to couch a letter. I would write maybe twenty letters a day for her, type them, and then give them to her to sign at night. This was her personal mail and a great way to learn about letter writing!

The press was brutal to her at times. One day someone wrote the most terrible article on her. Now, Clare made a practice of writing a nice note to everybody who wrote about her.

But this time I said, "How can I write a nice note to this horrible journalist?"

She said, "Write it. You never know what's going to happen the next time."

So I wrote a nice letter saying, "Thank you so much for the

long article about me and I'm sure that we will learn a great deal from your appraisal of my efforts..." She would end by writing, "When you come through Rome, do let me know."

I had been ready to poison that unfair journalist, but you know, the next article that came out on her in that newspaper was the feature center-cut and it was fabulous. So she knew, she knew. (He also visited her in Rome!)

She didn't, of course, speak any Italian for the first year, so I had the whole staff, twenty-two people, to cope with, and, believe me, there was a lot of volatility in that staff. The third day I was there, I heard shrieks, yelling, and pounding down below. I rushed down to the kitchen and I found the chef and the maitre d'hotel going at each other with kitchen knives. That's when I realized I was in for a real ride with this job. In any case, I got the knives out of their hands and calmed their Mediterranean tempers.

The Italians came to know Clare and they loved her; her staff loved her; the people in the streets loved her. We had to train everyone to say "ambasciatore," not "ambasciatrice." She wasn't an ambassador's wife, she was *the* ambassador, so in addressing her, one said, "Signor Ambasciatore." I had a lot of educating to do even among members of the diplomatic corps.

The Luces were among the first ambassadors ever to bring their personal art treasures to embellish the embassy residence. Mr. Luce's Ming and Tang camels and horses and their Old Masters and Impressionist paintings were extraordinary. It knocked the Italians' eyes out—Americans who were true art lovers!

Mrs. Luce dazzled me with her beauty, wardrobe, and jewels, although her fashion sense completely missed its mark at times. She had one particular dress made six times a year in different fabrics because she loved it. It was comfortable with long loose sleeves and a deep pocket on each side. She'd put her hands in the pockets, along with her glasses, pencils, compact, and everything else.

> My Christmas present was a pair of beautiful, little gold earrings studded with diamonds, and she said, "Now you have your diamonds, now you can marry for love."

Everything was custom made for her, but she hated fittings. She refused even to have them. She had a German maid named Gretel Steinfeld. Gretel was tall, thin, and stooped, and had a totally different figure from Mrs. Luce.

But Gretel had to go and stand in for the ambassador at the fittings. The poor Italian designer would have to look at Gretel and then refer to the ambassador's measurements on a piece of paper. "Hips, four inches wider; bust, four inches bigger; length, three inches shorter." In other words, every measurement had to be radically changed. And, of course, when these gorgeous dresses, including multi-thousand dollar evening ball gowns, arrived, they'd all have to be remade.

She wore beautiful perfume, and lots of it. She mixed them together and made her own scent. She liked Joy by Patou, and Pois de Senteur by Caron.

You knew when Clare Luce had been close by, by smelling the air in an embassy or a palazzo or wherever.

And jewels! I loved to look at them, and she loved to get them out and let me look at them. She didn't really appreciate them herself, but she enjoyed having somebody else appreciate them. I remember one day I said, "I must marry a rich man. I must have a taste of this in my life." She said sternly, "*Don't* do it! Don't ever do that." She had married first a rich man, George Brokaw, and it was a miserable match. "Don't ever ever marry for money," she commanded. That was in October. The following Christmas, my Christmas present was a pair of beautiful, little gold earrings studded with diamonds, and she said, "Now you have your diamonds, now you can marry for love."

That's the way she was. Those are some of the personal sides of this woman that you never heard about; you just heard about a powerful woman with an unpardonable temper.

Both Harry and Clare Luce were fascinated by my lifestyle. I was having all this fun fueled by endless energy. Mrs. Luce worked me until 9 o'clock every night. I would rush back to the apartment, change, and hurry out again at 10 o'clock with my Italian friends. We'd go over to the old part of Rome, *Trastevere*, have a superb dinner for the equivalent of two dollars, and take our *fiaschi* of wine with us to the top of the *Gianicolo* hill. There we would sit, all Romans (except for me), overlooking the city, and singing Neopolitan and Roman love songs, and strumming two or three guitars, and enjoying the vino. Simple romantic pleasures! I would have to tell the Luces about it the next day, because I was always asked, "What did you do last night?" I did all the fun things they couldn't do and wouldn't do, but would have liked to be young enough to want to do.

> **We had the greatest parties the Romans had ever seen.**

Harry Luce got so tired of hearing me rave about the soccer games (futbol), he insisted I take him along with my friends on Sunday to the Foro Romano for the match. Very emotional! The stadium was filled with thousands of screaming Italians, while Mr. Luce looked distinguished in his gray Chesterfield, and very bewildered, too. At one point, the people behind us got so excited, they smashed his gray fedora right down over his ears.

There's no question but that Clare used her beauty and her sex appeal for political gain. It was great to watch her.

On one occasion, she came up against a powerful communist minister who was rigidly opposed to her, a strong man, and she was determined to win him over. She invited him for drinks one night. (Harry Luce was back in New York.) She had a ruse. I used to sing Italian songs and play the guitar. So I got on the top of the stairway, got out my guitar, and played and sang a love song. She was up there with me, and he was waiting at the bottom of the stairs for her. When I finished, she sauntered down the stairway, holding my guitar. And she said, "Oh, Signor' Ministro, you're here."

He said, "Signor' Ambasciatore, was that you singing?"

"Of course." She gave him champagne. She was dressed in a black-sequined dress wearing this marvelous perfume and her jewels. For two hours, she really worked him over. Let me tell you, that ministro changed some of his political emotions that night.

One day, the Luces said, "Let's have those marvelous singers and guitarists and dancers come to perform at the villa for our official state dinners." So these wonderful Romani musicians, who'd never seen the insides of an embassy before, came and performed. They stunned the Roman aristocracy, the guests, the stuffy principessi and marchese. We had the greatest parties the Romans had ever seen.

Clare liked men. And in those days, whenever the dinner was finished, the women would peel off to a salon for a demitasse, or to powder their noses. She, of course, stayed behind with the men in the dining room, talking. She even stayed with the men after dinner in other people's homes, which shocked the Romans, but they finally got used to it and began to do it themselves.

Clare maintained that the best conversation is when people have had a good dinner and good wine. She wasn't going to let anything ruin that. She had all the men discussing her own choice of topics, and, of course, her own conversation was brilliant.

She had few close women friends, but the ones she had were very close. She also took care of many women friends—five that I was aware of—who had fallen on hard times. Some did not know that she was paying their rent, and their doctor bills. That was beautiful too.

She had dropped leaflets from a biplane for women's right to vote and done other things to help women, yet she was steadfastly against abortion. As grand and witty as she was, she could do anything she wanted to do.

Since Mr. Luce had no rank in Italy, the Italians didn't know what to do with him protocol-wise. They'd never had a husband of a high-ranking woman official to deal with in seating official dinners. But it couldn't have mattered less to him that he had no rank.

> She had all the men discussing her own choice of topics, and, of course, her own conversation was brilliant.

The first day I met him, he said, "Come on, I'll take you into the Villa Taverna entrance to the catacombs, I want to explore them myself." So we opened this creaking door in the garden into the catacombs, both armed with flashlights. It was cold, dark, and scary and after about ten minutes, I said, "Mr. Luce, I have to go back to the residence because the phone must be ringing constantly. Will you be all right?" He answered, "Of course."

So I went back to the door, and shut it without thinking. He was locked in for over an hour. Normally, anybody would have gotten fired for doing such a thing.

I loved him. He was always portrayed as a gruff, mean man, but to me he was a sweetie-pie, even when he'd blow up at me, which he did regularly. One time, he angrily accused me of having taken his *Rome Daily American*, the local newspaper, and I said, "Mr. Luce, I have not touched it."

He said, "There's only one person who could have taken it. It's you," and he went off fuming and furious.

About two hours later, Henry Luce's secretary called me, saying, "You spoke the other day to the Luces about the shoemaker, Dal'co, who custom makes these new satin pumps, with rhinestone heels, the most exquisite things you've ever seen." In those days, that kind of shoe was unheard of. The secretary then said, "Go to Dal'co this afternoon and custom order yourself a pair." Harry Luce had felt embarrassed about accusing me of taking his *Rome Daily American*, and so he made me a present of those pumps. That's the kind of person he was.

You know, JFK was the same way. He used to get mad and tear my head off and then feel badly about it, and I'd get a note from him saying, "I really made a mistake, please forgive me." That's what great people do. Great people lose their temper, often and justifiably, but you must understand that it's the pressure of their job that makes them behave that way, and you forgive them. You absorb some of the pressure they live with.

But back to Clare. Clare Luce was an incredible collector of gadgets and gimmicks. She had every electronic device known to man. But nothing would ever work because it was always made for the American system of voltage.

So we had generators sent over by the dozens. They all blew immediately. There she'd be in the middle of the bedroom, totally frustrated, saying, "Do something about it!" But I didn't know anything about electric matters. I'll always remember her generators blowing and all of her electronic stuff going kaflooey.

SHE WORKED OUT OF HER BED ALL THE TIME. It was fitted with luxurious satin sheets. She had pockets hanging from her side of the mattress for her extra glasses, pens, pencils, and notepads.

She was the most organized person I ever knew. When I asked her, "Why do you work in bed all the time?" she said, "Well, remember, whatever thinking you can do off your feet and in bed, is going to be superior to what you do on your feet." Now I do my best work in bed, too!

The Luces were great hosts and she expected me to make her parties memorable. I remember the first time I did a really important menu—it was for a dinner for Ezra Taft Benson, then the secretary of agriculture. He later became a senior elder of the Mormon Church.

The Bensons came to Rome for a big conference and were the guests of honor at an important dinner hosted by the Luces. Both Ambassador Luce and Mr. Luce noted that their guests of honor didn't touch their food, so they decided they must have stomach problems from their long travels. They asked if they could get some medication for them, but discovered the reason for their abstinence. It was because of my menu. Mormons don't touch alcohol, and I had sherry in the consomme, white wine in the fish course, red wine in the meat sauce, and cognac in the Crème Brulee dessert.

Mr. Luce said, "You know, Tish, if you had tried for ten years to come up with a menu that was more inappropriate than that, you couldn't have succeeded."

Clare had a great sense of PR, and did I ever learn about public relations. When her little dog, Scusi, had two little babies and died in childbirth, the vet said, "These pups are going to die if you don't find the perfect nursing mother."

So we asked all around Rome, even the zoo and all the vets, and finally, somebody suggested I go to the Canile Communale, the worst dog pound imaginable. I went there and found a scroungy mongrel wolfhound who had just had eight big pups, but she looked sweet, so I bought her for a couple of dollars, had her deflead and debugged, and brought her to the Villa Taverna.

Clare Luce was waiting for us with an empty box for canned soup from the PX, in which she had put a blanket to make a little home for the pups. So Signora Dog settled herself in the box, pulled in her own pups, and nursed ours for weeks. She literally saved their lives.

When this miracle happened, Clare tenderly touched the mangy dog and said, "I christen you Signora Snackbar," then addressing the two tiny puppies, "and I christen you Romulus and Remus." The press had a field day, headlining the news with, "Italian heroine solves desperate U.S. Embassy crisis," and the like.

On another occasion, when the ambassador joyfully accepted the admiral's invitation to make an official visit to the U.S. fleet in Naples, a limousine and naval escort were dispatched to bring her from Rome to Naples. She had outwitted them, having secretly arranged to be picked up at the Rome airport by a U.S. navy jet fighter pilot, and depositied on the flight deck of the *S.S. Forrestal*. With the entire navy hovering around the aircraft carrier and with many hundreds of naval personnel on deck, she climbed out of the fighter plane clad in a hot orange jumpsuit, designed for the occasion by the famed *sarto* Fabioni. Her sense of drama inevitably resulted in a smashing public relations gesture!

Grateful for her welcome by the fleet in Naples, she invited the navy to the Villa Taverna gardens for the annual Fourth of July celebration. Nearly a thousand sailors came, trampled over the roses, drank what seemed like tons of lemonade, and consumed thousands of hot dogs and ice cream bars, all paid for by the Luces' generous pockets. (The U.S. budget for the Fourth of July party allowed only for sodas.)

We soon realized we didn't have any portable johns, so we had to open one door of the villa to enable people to use the bathroom. This powder room had beautiful objects on the dressing table. I never thought about it but those beautiful objects were suddenly no longer there after the party was over. I had the unhappy task of reporting to Mrs. Luce that her priceless Faberge dressing table set had been stolen.

Clare reported it to the admiral, and the admiral said, "Don't worry, Mrs. Luce, you'll have them back very soon." And by George, two days later, a car arrived from Naples with the beautiful dressing table set in a box. I asked, "How did this happen, how did you find whoever took it?"

The naval officer replied, "It's just a mystery."

But I found out later that the admiral had told everybody in naval operations that they were going to lose a number of days of leave if they couldn't produce that dressing table set. It was a surefire way of unmasking the culprits!

My historic faux pas continued. The new Pakistan ambassador was to be the guest of honor at a huge reception at the Villa Taverna along with the entire diplomatic corps and major government officials. Pakistan was a new military ally and very important to us. Ambassador Luce was instructed by Washington to pull out all the stops. The Pakistan ambassador arrived but didn't speak any Italian. I had to introduce him to the assembled guests—and I introduced him to one and all as the ambassador from India. Pakistan and India were at war on their borders, of course, at this moment.

When the ambassador found out how I was introducing him, he stormed out of the residence, mortally insulted. Then Ambassador Luce said to me, "Listen, this is your fault, I had nothing whatsoever to do with it. It's entirely up to you to get us out of it."

I called the Pakistan Embassy and couldn't get through. I sent the ambassador a letter by hand; he wouldn't read it. I sent him another letter the next day; he wouldn't read it. Finally, in desperation, I got a dozen beautiful red roses, and had the chauffeur take them with a note from me saying, "I am so sorry that I did this. It's all my fault, I'm so sorry." He called me on the phone and I heard a smile in his voice. "I cannot resist a young woman sending me roses," he said. "You're forgiven."

I owe so much to Clare Boothe Luce. She was my inspiration, my mentor, and above all, my friend. A woman like her comes along once in a century. How lucky I was to have been in her path! ■

SEXUALLY TRANSMIT-
TED DISEASES OFTEN
DISPLAY FEW SYMP-
TOMS, BUT THEY CAN LEAD TO
INFERTILITY AND EVEN CERVI-
CAL CANCER. AS YOU MAY
KNOW, CERVICAL CANCER IS
ON A TREMENDOUS INCREASE.
—ELAYNE BENNETT

CHARACTER *Can Be* TAUGHT

BY ELAYNE BENNETT
WASHINGTON, D.C., MARCH 24, 2000
EXCERPTS FROM A SPEECH AT THE CONSERVATIVE WOMEN'S NETWORK

PLATO, IN HIS DIALOGUES, ASKS, "Can Virtue or Character Be Taught?" In America, we have consistently answered yes to that question. The belief that moral values should be taught to the young is as old as the republic itself. The history books tell us Thomas Jefferson insisted on the equal importance of intellectual and moral fortification. And that Abigail Adams gracefully reminded her son, John Quincy, that he must have good character before all else. (We can only wish Virginia Clinton had followed her lead.)

Remember too that the primary purpose behind the establishment of the American system of public education was to instill in boys and girls of different backgrounds and nationalities shared moral purposes and aspirations. We haven't changed. When given a list of dozens of goals for public education, American parents continue to stress two: to teach our

children how to read and write and count, and think correctly; and to help them develop a reliable sense of right and wrong.

ELAYNE BENNETT is the president and founder of Best Friends Foundation, a nonprofit organization that works with adolescent girls to educate them about abstinence through critical thinking and fitness activities. She lives in Maryland with her husband, William, and two sons.

Webster has a number of definitions for the word "character," including "morality or moral fiber, honesty, integrity, uprightness, decency, respectability, honor, courage, and goodness." These are the qualities we want to see in our young people.

Perhaps the effect of not promoting character in our youth today is felt more deeply than ever before. In poll after poll, American people have identified moral decline and its impact on the physical and moral safety of our children as our greatest national concern.

Back in 1987, I was working with adolescent girls at the Georgetown University Child Development Center, which is part of the hospital. As an educator, I had studied child development, and later I supervised and trained teachers. Along the way I realized that while there was a great deal of programmatic activity in early childhood and infant development, around about ages ten, eleven, and twelve, things slacked off pretty dramatically.

Observing babies being evaluated for serious developmental deficits, I'd see that the age of the mother was fifteen, sixteen, and seventeen. Within only two or three months, I noted that the ages of the mothers had dropped to fourteen, thirteen, twelve, and even a few eleven-year-olds, most from a low socio-economic level.

At the other end, girls from upper-class and middle-class households were suffering from depression, anxiety, in some cases suicidal tendencies, and they had been referred for therapy. These girls often stated that a love relationship gone sour was at the root of their problem. The girls were devastated when the guy left, in most cases after having sex with him.

It occurred to me that these troubled girls and girls in trouble, although from very different backgrounds, were all lacking one thing—guidance and strength of character. No one, it appeared, had really talked to them about life and love, and no one was talking to them about self-respect or self-control.

In poll after poll, American people have identified moral decline as our greatest national concern.

I believed that those girls would benefit from participating in a positive peer group guided by responsible women. And so, I began to think through an educational curriculum based on the concept of girls supporting one another, under the guidance of older women, but with one thing in common: they were all going to say that sexual intercourse is wrong for teenagers.

When I began, I resolved to have an achievable concrete goal, to take one small step at a time. We should ask the girls to wait at least until high school graduation before having sex—a definable goal. We wanted to see if this would work.

Remember, this was 1987, and there was no talk at all about abstinence. It was a given that teenagers were going to have sex. It was a given that they must protect themselves. It was all about sex plus contraception. Ours was a pretty revolutionary idea.

I decided to have a field test at Langley High School in Virginia, with one of the most demanding county school boards in the country. We were put through the mill. We showed a little snippet of a video I had seen on *Good Morning America* in 1987. It was called, "How Can I Tell If I'm Really in Love?" It intrigued me because one of the messages was "sex is not the same as love." I ended up negotiating with high-level attorneys at Paramount from my kitchen, as I watched my two-year-old in the sandbox. This was because Bill mentioned to me one day, "You know, you've probably violated some copyright laws somewhere." In the end, the lawyers gave us an edited version for classroom use; we use the video to this day.

And so we developed a curriculum on love and dating, starting with that first video, and field tested it at Langley High School during a three-hour a day for three days health seminar.

At the end, 73 percent of the girls said yes, they would like to be part of a group in which girls supported each other in waiting to have sex. And another 85 percent said yes, this was the right message, but... When we flipped through their evaluations we found such messages as, "It's too late for me, start younger." These girls were finishing tenth grade; they were fifteen. One girl wrote, "My sister is only 12, and she's receiving pressure." Another one wrote, "Sometimes I think the only reason girls do have sex is because of pressure from peers and lack of guidance from adults." Amazingly, the girls were actually asking for adult guidance.

Soon afterward, I presented my findings to a group of educators at the U.S. Department of Education—I happened to know the guy who was secretary (my husband, Bill Bennett). By the way, use every means you have to make headway. I used my husband, I will admit. I cannot stress how important that is.

I found out that the department had adopted a school program begun in the Reagan administration. Various departments of government would adopt a school, which was generally in their neighborhood, and people from the Department of Justice, HUD or Education would tutor in the schools.

As it turned out, Amidon Elementary in Southwest Washington was the adopted school of the U.S. Department of Education, and I began teaching poetry, writing, and rhyming songs, in the first through fifth grades.

I became friendly with the principal, Pauline Hamlette, and invited her to a meeting of educators where I planned to present the Best Friends model for their reactions. Interestingly, several women stood up—I think they were Ph.Ds, and they were white—and said, "Well, it's a good idea, but you can't take this idea into the inner city. They're not going to listen to you. It's a different culture."

I stood there thinking, "Well, perhaps they're right, they're Ph.Ds; they must know everything." Then Pauline Hamlette stood up—Pauline is a statuesque, lovely black woman—and she said, "That's not true. Children know when you really care about them." And she said, "I've seen Mrs. Bennett in the classroom. These kids know if someone's a phony or for real. She's for real— she really cares about them." And she said, "I want this program next year, and I want to start it in the sixth grade." And that was when we took off.

We left Fairfax County Schools, with all the money and all the talented children, all of whom said start younger; and we ended up starting in the sixth grade in a poor section of Washington, D.C. And we followed this group of girls through junior and senior high school.

Since then, more than a thousand girls in D.C. public schools, and more than five thousand girls nationally, have participated in the program.

Today, we have sixty girls who are in college on Best Friend scholarships. As a result of early tutoring, good character education, and discussion about some of the real issues in life, we have this year a freshman at Stanford, a sophomore at Temple, two girls at the University of Pennsylvania, one at the University of North Carolina, two at Cornell, and on and on. We also have forty girls eligible for college. We have a number of girls whose SAT scores are in the 1100 to 1200 range, a really extraordinary achievement. In our early years, we rarely saw a total score over 900.

A word about counseling. We ask the girls to meet with us during semester break, holiday break. We talk them through their course selections, their problems. One girl at Emory wanted to be a physician. But her advisor said, "No, you need to rethink this. You really don't want to go into medicine because it's for white men. You don't stand a chance."

So we sat down and wrote a nice letter to the advisor explaining that this young woman needed a chance. She is currently in med school.

What then is Best Friends? It is an educational program that addresses moral character by fostering self-respect and promoting self-control. Our program is based on the true spirit of friendship: adolescent girls discussing their problems, desires, and dreams with one another, and helping each other make difficult but sound decisions.

We emphasize the joy of preteen years, years free from the

complications of sexual activity. We provide guidance and skills that adolescent girls need to lead happy and responsible lives. We do not employ scare tactics. We're positive; our message is upbeat; we have no political agenda or religious affiliation. We are in the public schools and we've had no problem with our message.

> **We emphasize the joy of preteen years, years free from the complications of sexual activity.**

Among the thousand Washington, D.C., girls who participated in the program for two years, only three have reported pregnancies—out of one thousand girls!—and consistently less than 10 percent have used drugs.

During the last school year, 2,600 Best Friends girls nationally were evaluated with our anonymous self-report. There were eighteen pregnancies—less than a 1 percent pregnancy rate nationally. We discovered that 5 percent of the 2,600 said they had had sexual intercourse; 9 percent had been sexually abused. Sexual abuse is another whole area that desperately needs attention. As many as five girls out of twenty-five in an elementary fifth grade class have reported sexual abuse.

When Best Friends began, there was a 26 percent rate of pregnancy in D.C. schools—so a little over one out of every four girls became pregnant in the D.C. public schools before graduating. That percentage has dropped to 18 percent. And it is not because of increased contraception, as touted by Planned Parenthood.

A recent study from *Child Trends* magazine reported that an increased number of girls used contraception at their first intercourse. But what has received very little attention is that research has demonstrated that girls have decreased their use of contraception after repeated sexual activity. It is not likely that pregnancy will result from first intercourse, so why did the pregnancy rate drop when girls reported less use of contraception? It would seem logical that the decrease in the pregnancy rate is due to something else. We think it is because the abstinence message is catching on.

Another interesting fact: Nationally, 77 percent of the girls polled said they wanted to wait until after high school to have sex. But another figure showed that 75 percent said they wanted to wait until marriage to have sex. This hardly jibes with the claims of our liberal friends that teenagers, or young people, would never entertain the idea of waiting until marriage to have sex.

Incidentally, our girls are not from intact families or have wonderful home lives; nearly 30 to 50 percent have been offered illegal drugs, but only 3 percent said they used them. Four percent of the Best Friends girls in Washington, D.C., reported using illegal drugs. Now compare that, 4 percent, in Washington out of our one thousand girls in all the nine wards of the city. Actually, our largest concentration in schools is in Ward 8, Anacostia, which is the area everybody has all but given up on.

On the health front, we need to remember that at age fifteen a sexually active girl has a one in eight chance of contracting a sexually transmitted disease. A twenty-one-year-old woman has a one in eighty chance.

So, if one has difficulty with the moral argument, one can

certainly make the public health argument. Physicians are greatly frightened because we have five or six new sexually transmitted diseases for which there is no cure and no treatment. We also know that the human papilloma virus, HPV, which causes genital warts, is transmitted through oral sex. It is not—I repeat, not—prevented by condom use.

And genital warts are also incurable. They may go into remission, but they're incurable. Sexually transmitted diseases often display few symptoms, but they can lead to infertility and even cervical cancer. As you may know, cervical cancer is on a tremendous increase.

I am not going to go into the drug issue, but believe me, the drug war was over in the Clinton administration. They abandoned it. Today, more drugs than ever are available. If I may quote my husband: "Never before have drugs been so available, and never before have they been so cheap, and never before have they been so pure..." We have great hope in our new drug czar, John Walters, recently nominated by George W. Bush.

Let me close by saying that we know in our hearts that the message of Best Friends—abstinence from sex, drugs, and alcohol—is a message young people are waiting to hear. We believe each girl has something positive to offer our society if given the opportunity to develop her potential. And we welcome everyone's participation as a parent, as a community member, or as a mentor. ■

YOUNG PEOPLE TODAY DON'T HAVE MUCH TRUST IN THE FEDERAL GOVERNMENT. THE YOUNG ARE ALSO SUSPICIOUS OF BIG BUSINESS. AND MANY DISTRUST THE INSTITUTION OF MARRIAGE.

— KARLYN BOWMAN

How Women See Themselves: *The Latest Polls*

BY KARLYN BOWMAN
WASHINGTON, D.C., MAY 12, 2000
EXCERPTS FROM A SPEECH AT THE CONSERVATIVE WOMEN'S NETWORK

TO TALK ABOUT ATTITUDES OF WOMEN is a very big subject, and I propose to paint with a broad brush.

A good place to begin today is with a Gallup poll that was conducted in 1946. That year Gallup asked men and women separately about opportunities for their sons and daughters. They asked mothers whether the opportunities for their daughters would be better than the ones that they had and fathers about opportunities for their sons.

Virtually identical portions, about 60 percent of men, and 60 percent of women, expected that the opportunities for their sons and daughters would be better than the ones they had had. That's a very familiar finding in public opinion; we tend to be optimistic about our prospects—it's part of the way we define ourselves as a nation.

Gallup didn't repeat that question until 1997. And in that year, the results were quite interesting. Roughly 60 percent of men said, once again, that

KARLYN BOWMAN is a resident fellow at the American Enterprise Institute and a senior editor for the institute's flagship magazine, *The American Enterprise*. She writes widely about public opinion and demographics. She lives with her husband Jim in Alexandria, Virginia.

their sons' opportunities would be better than the ones they had had. But the mothers' optimism about their daughters had soared: 85 percent of women said they believed that their daughters would have a better life than they had had.

It's hard for many of you here to realize how different attitudes were just twenty-five or thirty years ago, a single generation. In 1969, for example, for the first time in polling history, a majority, 55 percent, approved of a married woman earning money in business or industry if she had a husband capable of supporting her. And in the early 1970s, about 45 percent agreed that most men are better suited emotionally for politics than are most women.

The idea that women should be given full equality of status is, of course, a natural element of the socio-political individualism that defines us as a nation. By contrast, in societies that are based on class or hereditary ideas, the difference in men's and women's roles are seen as immutable and natural, and changes have been more often denied.

Today in the United States, women tell the pollsters that the jobs available to them, their salaries, their opportunities for leadership have improved since the 1970s.

But women here are divided, and on many questions, downright pessimistic, about whether life has improved in terms of their roles as homemakers, mothers, and in the kind of marriages that they have. Only slightly more than a third say that their lives have improved in those dimensions since the 1970s.

Japanese women, by contrast, live in a traditional, patriarchal society. They also see progress in terms of opportunities, salaries, and jobs that are available to them. But they are much more likely than American women to see progress in their marriages and their home lives.

The puzzle is explained this way; we are much farther along than the Japanese in terms of expanding individualism and extending opportunities for women, and therefore, we're the first to experience and confront the problems that those new opportunities create.

> When societies agree on ends, most people tend to disengage from the discussion about the *means* by which those ends will be accomplished.

Given our history, I don't think it's surprising that a majority of women in the 1999 Roper Starch Worldwide poll told interviewers that because women have more choices today they have a greater chance of being happy. But a solid 25 percent disagreed, saying that more choices simply made life more complicated.

Forty percent of women in that same poll said that their expanded choices had made life more difficult for men; only 36 percent said it provided men with more opportunities.

In the late 1960s and the early 1970s, we as a society generally agreed that women should be provided full opportunities to participate. We agreed on the *ends* that policy should serve. When societies agree on ends, most people tend to disengage from the discussion about the *means* by which those ends will be accomplished. Thus it's not surprising that a CBS poll from 1997, thirty-five years after the heyday of feminism, found that only 43 percent said that the women's movement had achieved anything to make their lives easier; 48 percent said it had not. Just 28 percent told Yankelovich Partners in 1998 that feminism today was relevant to them personally—a third of young women gave that response. Fifty-six percent of women in the poll were not familiar with Gloria Steinem; and only 50 percent of self-identified feminists were familiar with her. Today, only around 30 percent of women call themselves feminists.

Because of the success of the women's movement, most women have turned their attention to other things. Many social movements and organizations find it difficult to thrive, once their goals are generally adopted. Organized feminism doesn't interest most women today. Let me now relate some recent findings about how women see themselves.

Huge majorities say that women do not face discrimination in getting a college education. They say that their salaries are generally equal to those of the men they work with.

Nearly six in ten, however, say that women are discriminated against in getting executive positions or top government jobs. Although men and women say that they would vote for a qualified woman for president, majorities of women still believe that many Americans aren't ready to elect a woman.

Women who work say that their jobs are essential in bringing in income for their families, not simply as money for extras.

Women with children who work outside the home, feel that they're balancing their work and their family lives pretty well. When asked what would make life better, twice as many women mention more money than mention anything else, such as "family friendly" workplaces.

Although women as a whole are divided about whether they prefer to stay home or have a job, a strong majority of working women say that they prefer to work outside the home. (Interestingly, more men than in the past are saying that they would prefer to stay home.)

When most women are asked whether they consider their work a career, or just a job, 44 percent of American women describe their work as a career, but 53 percent as just a job. Seventy-five percent of college grads described their work as a career, compared to 14 percent of non-high school grads, 28 percent of high school grads, and 39 percent of those with some college. Young employed women are more likely than any other group to see their work as just a job.

Perhaps because they believe discrimination still exists for top jobs, women think that their best chances for success are in starting their own business.

Most women and men say that they want to marry, and most in fact, will. The number of never-marrieds in the population was 23 percent in 1950; it's about 28 percent today. But in all the surveys I've seen since 1970, men and women think that the institution of marriage is much weaker than it was ten to fifteen years ago. They feel that same way about religion.

Most people describe their marriages as happy and say they'd marry the same person again.

Husbands and wives disagree most about what TV programs to watch, who controls the remote, and how much to save and spend. Four in ten women say that their spouse really believes that housework is a woman's responsibility, and that he's doing her a favor by helping out; 54 percent of women disagree.

A near majority of women tell the pollsters that they are a lot more knowledgeable than their mothers about making financial decisions. Just a third of men say that they are more knowledgeable than their fathers about financial affairs.

In 1968 just 28 percent of young white women expected that they would be working at age thirty-five. More than 70 percent of them found themselves working in their thirties. Most young women today expect to work in their thirties.

When we're asked what we daydream about, 44 percent say about winning the lottery, 43 percent about having no stress in our lives, and 42 percent about being rich. Only 3 percent of women say they daydream about being elected to political office.

I'd like to turn to the attitudes of young people, and particularly young women in the eighteen to twenty-nine-year-old group, because they are very different from their older brothers and sisters in the Baby Boom generation. The surveys show something that is heartening for conservatives, because young people often lead change.

When asked what they want to be when they grow up, many young people give familiar responses: doctors, lawyers, teachers. But today many young people are saying that they want to start their own small businesses. We are seeing a reaffirmation of a very old virtue, and that is self-reliance.

Young people today don't have much trust in the federal government. Frank Luntz, a top pollster, did a poll a while ago, which showed that more young people believed they'd see a UFO than that they'd see their Social Security checks.

The young are also suspicious of big business. They've seen layoffs and downsizing in their own families and communities. And even though most of them say they want to marry, many distrust the institution of marriage. A quarter of the eighteen to twenty-nine-year-olds are now products of divorce.

So we have a generation that is much more skeptical of big institutions than in the past, and knows it will have to be more self-reliant. This is one of the reasons George Bush's discussion of partial privatization of Social Security will reach a very receptive audience. Young people are confident that they are going to have to rely on themselves as they grow older.

Most young women say that they want to marry and to have families, but they're not sure they will be able to realize that, their ideal. We don't have any good data about whether or not they'd like to work for a while, take some time off, and then go back into the workforce, or whether they plan to work all along. We need more time to see what young people are really saying about family and worklife. But this generation is

going to be significantly different from the Baby Boom generation.

They may not have a big impact on this election campaign,
because young people don't tend to vote at the same rates as
their elders do. The survey data suggest that when you have
more of a stake in society—when you are married, have a
mortgage and children—you tend to be more prone to vote.

To wrap up, women as a whole are optimistic about many
aspects of their lives, but pessimistic about some, in part
because they have so many more opportunities than in the
past, and are the first to deal with the problems that all these
new opportunities provide. ■

(Portions of this talk have appeared in articles by the author.)

WE'VE REALLY REACHED A PERIOD IN OUR HISTORY WHEN WE HAVE TO DECIDE WHETHER OR NOT WE WANT TO BECOME A BALKANIZED NATION, WITH LOTS OF LITTLE INDIVIDUAL ETHNIC AND RACIAL GROUPS, WHETHER WE WANT DIVERSITY TO OVERSHADOW WHAT WE HAVE IN COMMON. IN THE PAST, OUR GREAT SUCCESS AS A NATION WAS OUR ABILITY TO TAKE PEOPLE FROM EVERYWHERE ACROSS THE GLOBE AND MAKE AMERICANS OF THEM.

—LINDA CHAVEZ

THE NEW AMERICA:

Has the Melting Pot Boiled Over?

BY LINDA CHAVEZ
WASHINGTON, D.C., JULY 23, 2001
EXCERPTS FROM A SPEECH AT THE CONSERVATIVE WOMEN'S NETWORK

THE WHOLE TOPIC OF IMMIGRATION has fascinated me for many years. Although my book, *Out of the Barrio*, was published in 1991, it was clear back in the 1980s that something was happening in the United States in terms of its demographics, and that it was having a rather profound effect on American life. And now, just recently, the Census Bureau reports that there are more than 35 million Hispanics in the United States. And the Hispanic population is only part of the foreign-born population of the United States.

Today we are experiencing a level of immigration that is the second-highest in our nation's history, the highest occurring between 1900 and 1924. This has concerned many people. They want to know whether this will mean a substantial change in who we are as a nation and who we are as a people.

In the aftermath of the civil rights movement—and even more so, the affirmative action movement—we hear a great deal about the importance of

LINDA CHAVEZ is president of the Center for Equal Opportunity. She writes a weekly syndicated column, is a political analyst for FOX News channel, and authored *Out of the Barrio: Toward a New Politics of Hispanic Assimilation*. The mother of three grown sons, she lives in Virginia with her husband.

racial and ethnic diversity, our new primary values, what sep-arates us from each other, what makes us unique.

Back in the late eighties, when I was writing my book and looking for information about the Hispanic population, it seemed to me that the picture of Hispanics I was getting when I turned on the television or opened the newspaper wasn't meshing with my own experience. I grew up at a time in America when there was substantial prejudice and discrimina-tion against blacks, Mexican-Americans, and others.

When I was growing up in Denver, Colorado, and my mother, a blue-eyed blonde whose maiden name was McKenna, applied for a job, she was told, "Yes, we're going to hire you, but we're going to call you by your first name." She became "Miss Lou," because the clientele of the store would not be comfortable being served by someone named Mrs. Chavez.

But today—despite reading that that bias has continued—if I were to go to the same store where my mother worked, it would likely have a Mrs. Ramirez or a Mrs. Sanchez or a Mrs. Chavez, not just as a salesperson, but as the head of the divi-sion or even as a vice president of the company.

Even more, in doing research for my book, I would read sta-tistics that one out of every two Hispanics dropped out of school, that Hispanics only earned about half what whites earned, that they were mainly uneducated, poor, and down-trodden, and that they would need substantial government assistance if they were to make it in this society. But again, this was not what I had seen and was experiencing. So I began to gather some statistics of my own.

The first thing I discovered was that the Hispanic population in the United States in 1960, according to the census records, was substantially smaller, and very different from today's. In 1960, 85 percent of Hispanics in the United States were American born. Many of them, like my

> Today we are experiencing a level of immigration that is the second-highest in our nation's history, the highest occurring between 1900 and 1924.

family, had been here for generations. My first family members came to what is now New Mexico in the year 1609. And they've been there ever since. Many more people could trace their families back, if not that far, at least to the turn of the century, many of them arriving after the Mexican revolutions in the first decades of the twentieth century.

The second thing that I noticed was that there had, in fact, been substantial changes in the population and substantial progress for those persons who were actually born here in the United States, but they were hidden. And they were hidden because in gathering statistics, we are obsessed with race and ethnicity. We're constantly asking people to check off boxes—what is your national origin, what is your race or ethnicity—and when we put all of the statistics together and regurgitate them in categories, we do it racially and ethnically, but not necessarily by dividing them in terms of where people were born. Recall that the immigration laws of the

United States were changed in the mid-1960s, and immigration changed its pattern in that decade and subsequently. Whereas previously the largest group of immigrants to the United States came from Europe, after the 1965 law was passed that shifted dramatically, and the largest number of immigrants—about 80 percent—since have come from two regions: Asia and Latin America.

In short, what I did when I wrote my book was to take the statistics and put a different filter on, to take a look at them depending on where the persons were born. And what I found was that among American-born Hispanics in the United States all the progress that I had seen and witnessed was real—people were, in fact, moving up into management positions. They were going to school, staying in school longer, getting college degrees, all reflected in their earnings. And they were earning substantially the same as non-Hispanic whites.

But the newcomer population—like the Italians and the Jews and the Greeks and the Poles and others who had come in the early 1900s—were starting off at the bottom levels of the economic ladder. They came here largely seeking more economic opportunity, and they were availing themselves of that opportunity once they got here. But, as with every immigrant group, it was taking time for them to move up that ladder.

When you look at the average Mexican immigrant to the United States in the census years I was studying—the 1980 census and some survey data from the late eighties—you will find that the average Mexican immigrant who entered the

United States had six years of education. Well, when you're a census taker and you find that the average person in a group has six years of education, it's going to have an enormous impact on your overall statistical snapshot. It comes out in the oft-quoted citation that about half of all Hispanics living in the United States do not complete high school.

But that doesn't adequately describe either the people born here or the newcomers. The people born here, by and large, stay in school and graduate from high school—about 80 percent of them, according to the most recent numbers, have high school degrees. And when you're talking about immigrants, most of them have not even made it into high school. But they haven't dropped out of American schools; they dropped out of schools before coming to the United States. And obviously, if you have only six years of education, that's going to affect your earnings ability. And it's going to limit your opportunities.

But these new immigrants also come with something else, something very important, almost as important as education, and that is the drive to succeed.

These Mexicans, after all, are largely people who have given up the security of living where they were born, have left their families and what was familiar to them—their neighborhoods, their towns, indeed, their country—and have sought a better life in a new place, with all of its challenges. They are highly motivated people. They are people who want to better themselves. And that motivation is reflected in some interesting statistics about what happens to them once they get here.

Which is that they are more likely to be members of the labor force than any other group in America, except for one, Haitian immigrants.

Both Mexicans and Haitians have labor force participation that exceeds that of whites and virtually all subgroups in the United States. They also are more likely to work more jobs and basically not to pass opportunity by. A number of years ago, a survey of employers asked whom they would rather hire for certain kinds of jobs, and these employers said they preferred immigrants to Americans, not because they could pay them less, which is a liberal allegation—exploiting immigrants— but because they show up for work every day, and on time, and if you hand them a broom and ask them to sweep the floor they don't give you a long dissertation about why it isn't their job to do so. That was the sort of snapshot reply they were getting in various forms over and over again. In contrast, the folks who come here show a strong willingness to work.

This rosy scenario of what's happening in respect to diversity suggests that there are no problems. Well, it's only a partial picture, because the United States to which these immigrants are coming is very different from the one that immigrants came to in the early 1900s. And the changes are largely due to public policy. We now have laws on the books that, I believe, will be a tremendous impediment to the ultimate integration of these newcomers, whether they be from China or from Mexico.

These laws fall into two categories. One is in the affirmative action arena, which, in my view, has been turned entirely on its head. It is no longer a program to open up opportunity for people who are the best qualified, regardless of their race, but a program granting preference on the basis of skin color. And that, of course, has destroyed the incentive to become part of the mainstream and part of the social fabric. Now we have a positive incentive to hold on to our racial and ethnic identity, *not* to integrate.

We now have laws on the books that, I believe, will be a tremendous impediment to the ultimate integration of these newcomers, whether they be from China or from Mexico.

But the second category is by far the single most important change in public policy, and that is education. In the past, when you came here from another country, the first thing you wanted to do was to learn English so that you could go on, get more education, land better jobs, and become part of the civic life of the nation. People were anxious to learn English. In the public schools of the early twentieth century in places like, say, the lower East Side of Manhattan, which was a virtual cauldron of different ethnicities and races, the first duty of the school was to teach children English.

Then in 1968 we passed a federal law that encouraged school districts to delay teaching English and to teach immigrants in their native language, particularly if that language was Spanish, and actually gave incentives to school districts to do so. Not surprisingly, as a result, learning English became a very hard thing to do. It gets even worse. In the public schools in places like California, Texas, Arizona, and elsewhere, there has actually been a mandate to teach these children in Spanish, and not just for a few weeks or a few months or even for a year or two, but for year after year after year. In California, the Los Angeles Unified School District, for one, mandated that newcomers be taught English for twenty minutes a day. Five hours a day, they'd be taught in Spanish. Well, guess what? If I spent twenty minutes a day trying to learn German, I wouldn't speak German very well, and these kids don't learn English either. This is not just a challenge to the immigrants, but a challenge to us.

In the past, our vision was clear—we were one nation and we were one people. Our national motto was "E pluribus unum"—"Out of many, one." We believed in trying to forge a common identity, that no matter where you came from, when you came to the United States you became part of the family. All that we really asked in return was that immigrants learn the language and accept the civil and civic obligations of the society—of a democratic society. That has been our tradition.

But that has become a thing of the past. We've really reached a period in our history when we have to decide whether or not we want to become a balkanized nation, with lots of little individual ethnic and racial groups, whether we want diversity to overshadow what we have in common. In the past, our great success as a nation was our ability to take people from everywhere across the globe and make Americans of them. In doing so we have forged a common identity, even though we might look different, might have different histories, and might have come from different places. That has been the great beauty of the United States.

But I don't believe that balkanized nations succeed. All you have to do is to see what is happening in the actual Balkans to know that balkanization doesn't work. So we need to reinvigorate the notion of one nation and one people. Language has been the glue that binds us together. And I believe that without emphasizing a common language, without emphasizing that we do expect newcomers to become part of our family, we will end up having a tremendous backlash. Americans who like the history and traditions of this country are going to say, "Okay, enough already. We're going to shut down the borders once and for all. We're not going to let newcomers in because we don't think they can assimilate."

I personally don't believe that. I believe that immigrants can assimilate and I believe that they want to assimilate. But the burden is on our shoulders; it is up to native-born Americans to recommit ourselves to the motto that created this nation, that we are one nation, that we are one people, and that what binds us together is much more important than what separates us into rival diverse groups. ■

Other countries have also seen wilderness designations or biosphere reserves virtually destroy the concept of private property.

—HELEN CHENOWETH-HAGE

Protecting Our Land Base

BY HELEN CHENOWETH-HAGE
WASHINGTON, D.C., JUNE 11, 1999
EXCERPTS FROM A SPEECH AT THE CONSERVATIVE WOMEN'S NETWORK

TODAY, A LARGELY OVERLOOKED but important subject has to do with our land base. For without the ability to own private property, there is no freedom. America has achieved the highest standard of living in history because America has had a gift of creativity that only comes from God. Being able to join that with the natural resources that we have in America resulted in what we call our original wealth. But unless these resources are mined or harvested, there is no original wealth.

The present expansion of the federal government, through a variety of different programs, is shrinking our private property, our land base. When we separate human beings from the land, when we are no longer able to mine, mill, or harvest, we are no longer able to create original wealth. And so our wealth resources continue to diminish, along with our freedom.

What few understand is that the federal land grab is tied into our national debt. It all started in the Johnson

HELEN CHENOWETH-HAGE represented Idaho in the U.S. House of Representatives from 1994 to 2000. Prior to her election she was a natural resources management consultant and guest instructor at the University of Idaho School of law. Nationally known for her work in lowering taxes and defending private property rights, she lives with her husband Wayne in Idaho.

administration when we allowed foreign investors to buy part of our debt. During these years, beginning in 1964, more and more of our land was set aside in various categories, such as wilderness and endangered species. Since all original wealth is derived from the land, what it boils down to is that the natural resources of this nation are being used as a collateral base for our national debt.

This situation is not unique to America. Other countries with a debt to the World Bank and various other international financial institutions have also seen wilderness designations or biosphere reserves virtually destroy the concept of private property.

Essentially, wealth in the form of property is being concentrated among fewer people because they are the ones who hold the paper, so to speak, for much of the collateralized land base. For example: When a huge wilderness area was set aside in Alaska in the early seventies, it was not by chance that the boundaries included very rich mineral reserves.

This philosophy is the antithesis of what America was founded on, which is, quite simply, the right of everyone—every American—to private ownership, whether it is your land, your home, your clothes, or your intellectual property. Remember: if the government can take your property, your land, it soon will reach into your bank account, your wallet.

We're already seeing examples of intellectual property being stolen. The worst is what the Red Chinese have recently taken from our nation. At this very moment, because of this

theft, twenty Red Chinese intercontinental ballistic missals are pointed at our
mainland. The technology to boost those
intercontinental rockets across the oceans
came from us, from our efforts. And, as
you know, one missile has multiple missile
heads which merve out and hit two or
three or four cities with a single launch.

If the government can take your property, your land, it soon will reach into your bank account, your wallet.

But back to private property. One insidious program that has
been eating away at our private property, as well as at our sovereignty as a nation, has come from the United Nations. It is
called the "American Heritage Sites" and the "Man and
Biosphere Reserves Sites."

As a freshman in Congress, I went one day to visit
Independence Hall in Philadelphia in order to see the Liberty
Bell. I discovered that the Liberty Bell is now incased in a
building that was built by the National Park Service. As I
stood in line waiting to go in, I noticed two plaques in the
brick walkways, one of which commemorated the site where
John Kennedy stood when he gave a speech for a certain occasion, a great tribute to a great patriot. I then went over to the
second plaque, which commemorated the dedication of this
site to the United Nations Educational, Scientific and Cultural
Organization, UNESCO. I was stunned—Independence Hall
was under the jurisdiction of UNESCO!

Realizing UNESCO uses one of two designations when tar-
geting a site for its control— (1) Rural Heritage Sites, and (2)

Biosphere Reserves—my staff and I did some research. We discovered that exactly forty-seven sites in America have been designated under the Man and Biosphere Reserve, and twenty sites have been designated as Rural Heritage Sites—all under the jurisdiction of UNESCO.

Among the sites designated as Biosphere Reserves are the Coast Ranges in California, Cascade Head in Oregon, the Central Gulf Coastal Plain in Florida, the Central Plains in Colorado, the Adirondacks in New York and Vermont, the Everglades in Florida, the New Jersey Pinelands, the Rocky Mountains in Colorado, the Three Sisters in Oregon, and Yellowstone National Park in Wyoming and Montana—and those are just a few examples of the stretch of the Biosphere Reserves. Among the twenty World Heritage Sites are the Carlsbad Caverns National Park, the Grand Canyon National Park, the great Smokey Mountains in Tennessee and North Carolina, the Hawaiian Volcanoes National Park, Independence Hall in Pennsylvania, the Liberty Bell, the Olympic National Park, the Statue of Liberty in New York, Yellowstone National Park, and Yosemite National Park—that is, our national heritage and national treasures.

After some studies, we found that all the land that has been taken—land given away by the government and currently under UN jurisdiction—would fill up the entire state of Colorado. Hundreds of thousands of American lives have been laid down, have been sacrificed to protect the sovereignty and land of our nation, and then our government just turns around and gives our land away; its jurisdiction has been handed over to others. This was too much.

In the buffer zone outside the Biosphere Reserve of Yellowstone National Park is a mine, which was being operated by a Canadian lease hold interest. They were planning on enlarging the mine and they submitted an environmental impact statement as required under the National Environmental Policy Act. They were three-quarters of the way through EIS, and all was in good order, when UNESCO marched in and condemned that private property—it was a patented mine, and therefore private property.

> Hundreds of thousands of American lives have been laid down, have been sacrificed to protect the sovereignty and land of our nation, and then our government just turns around and gives our land away.

That gave us the ammunition we needed to go to the congressional leadership and hold hearings on the resources committee. We brought representatives of the UN in front of us. I remember at one point asking UNESCO, in effect, "Where do you get this authority? As you may recall, Ronald Reagan pulled America out of UNESCO because of gross financial mismanagement on its part. What gives you the authority to come in and condemn American land?" And they couldn't answer except to say that the Clinton administration had invited them in. As a result, Representative Don Young, R-Alaska, and I put together a bill and ran it out on the floor of the House. Due to the support of the American people—from the East Coast to the West Coast—we were able to pass that bill by a huge majority.

But we couldn't find a hero in the Senate to back it. In my second term we ran the same bill again, and again failed in the Senate. But, believe me, we will keep right on trying.

UNESCO and our government have operated somewhat surreptitiously, to say the least. I want to read to you a few words from the UNESCO guidelines, the *Operational Guidelines for the Implementation of the World Heritage Sites*: "...to maintain the objectivity of the evaluation process and to avoid possible embarrassment to those concerned, state parties..." (To UNESCO, the United States of America is a "state party.")

But listen on. "State parties should refrain from giving undue publicity to the fact that a property has been nominated." And then, "Participation of the local people in the nomination process is essential to make them feel a shared responsibility with the state party, in the maintenance of the site..." They take the site, we maintain it. "But, this should not prejudice future decision making by the committee," the document continues.

They nominate the site, but they do not allow the participation of the property owner, and many times people don't even know that their private property is being nominated. Yet, Americans pick up the bill for the maintenance and expenses of the site.

(Incidentally, on the mine that was condemned; the American taxpayer had to pony up 66 million dollars to pay off the Canadian lease hold interest. And the woman who holds the patent received zero for her property as of the date of this speech.) Former UN Ambassador Jeane Kirkpatrick testified before our committee as follows: "The World Heritage and Man and the Biosphere committees make decisions affecting the land and the lives of Americans. Some of these decisions are made by representatives chosen by governments, not based on democratic representation, certainly not the representation in America. What recourse does an American have when the UN bureaucrats from Cuba or Iraq or Libya, all of which are parties to this treaty, have made a decision that uniquely damages his or her property rights that lie near a national park?"

The testimony was riveting. And the reaction against such encroachments on our liberties is growing and growing.

BUT NOW I WANT TO DEVIATE from my topic for just a couple of minutes. Our country has many problems. We in Congress are law-makers, we are not law enforcers. There is only so much we can do, those of us that have a heart for the Constitution and a love of liberty. One of those things is to appeal to almighty God for His intervention and His wisdom in the affairs of our country. Last January I was approached by eight pastoral leaders asking me to put together a resolution not only for a day of prayer, but for a day of prayer, fasting, and national repentance. As you may remember, Ronald Reagan set aside a national day of prayer in his first term.

We can no longer, however, set days aside in recognition of special events. We changed the rules in the House in 1995.

However, my resolution calls on the clergy of the United States, on business leaders, and on people across this nation to call for a solemn assembly, a national day of prayer and repentance. The Scriptures are pretty clear on this subject. In 2 Chronicles 7:14, it says, "If My people, who are called by My Name, seek My face, and turn from their wicked ways, and ask for forgiveness then I will give unto them and I will forgive their sins and I will heal their land."

God has made a covenant with His people and we have been a blessed nation; He has blessed us, continues to bless us with creative energy and great natural resources.

April 1863 was the last time that a call went out from the highest levels of government for a national day of prayer and fasting and repentance. Abraham Lincoln made that call when our nation was torn asunder by the great Civil War. Today our nation is being torn asunder spiritually. We cannot let this great country fall. With God's blessings on America, our land will be healed again. ■

Even though women consider themselves to be Democrat over Republican by eight points, women are twice as likely (45 percent-21 percent) to describe their social and economic outlook as "conservative" rather than "liberal."

—Kellyanne Conway

TRUTH IN POLLS: *How Junk Science Sustains the "Gender Gap"*

BY KELLYANNE CONWAY
WASHINGTON, D.C., OCTOBER 13, 2000
EXCERPTS FROM A SPEECH AT THE CONSERVATIVE WOMEN'S NETWORK

I'VE GOT GREAT NEWS TODAY—the "gender gap" is about to get its pink slip. The term, first popularized after the 1980 elections to describe the differences in voting preferences among men and women, has for two decades digressed from thoughtful discussion to use as a club against conservative candidates and causes.

The "gender gap" begins with a seemingly harmless, if not obvious, premise that men and women are different. Conservatives would agree, and celebrate those differences, since it was God, not a Republican or a Democrat, who first decided it should be so. It should surprise no one that men and women, who on balance think, behave, and respond differently to facts and circumstances, should do so as well at the ballot box.

As with many complex issues, the gender gap has been reduced by feminists and their pals in the media to a single issue: abortion.

KELLYANNE CONWAY (formerly Fitzpatrick) is CEO and president of the polling company(tm) and WomanTrend. She is an attorney, and has been a political analyst for several networks. Hours after delivering this address, she became engaged. Kellyanne resides with her husband, George, in Virginia and New York.

Conventional wisdom suggests that women vote Democratic and men vote Republican because of the parties' fundamental differences on the matter of abortion. This is simplistic, false, and insulting to women, since they process a panoply of matters before finalizing their political choices.

It is true that on balance voting women prefer Democratic candidates to Republican ones. To conclude that this flows directly from positions on abortion, however, is to confuse causation with coincidence. In fact, plenty of pro-life Republicans like Presidents Ronald Reagan and George H. W. Bush, have captured a majority of the women's vote, while avowedly pro-choice *female* Republican candidates have not, e.g., former New Jersey Governor Christine Whitman, who failed to garner 50 percent of the woman's vote in either of her statewide election victories.

The most important doubt about the prominence of abortion in voting comes from the women themselves. Even though women consider themselves to be Democrat over Republican by eight points, women are twice as likely (45 percent-21 percent) to describe their social and economic outlook as "conservative" rather than "liberal." Only one-fourth of women now consider themselves "feminists," a number that has been steadily declining for thirty years.

This is why, in my view, the major media play the debate between Republicans and Democrats rather than between conservatives and liberals. "Conservative" is a much more popular term than "Republican." But "Democrat" establishes a more positive identity than "liberal," even if it isn't an accurate indicator of most women's political opinions and ideologies.

A full 72 percent of women say that if their financial means allowed, they would stay home to raise their own children. My work has taken me to nearly every nook and cranny in this country, and I have yet to meet a loving mother who thinks, if given the option, that she could not or would not provide superior care to her child than a nanny or the Nanny State.

Palpable majorities of women support conservative prescriptions on key issues like school choice, crime and drugs, abstinence and adoption, and reductions in taxation and regulation.

The phrase "I am 100 percent pro-choice" no longer flows easily from the tongues of many women. In fact, an eye-popping 63 percent of women (and 59 percent of men) surveyed by the *Los Angeles Times* this year agreed with the statement "Abortion is murder" and a comparable number support making partial-birth abortion illegal.

The so-called hot button issues like abortion or equal rights are conspicuous by their absence in legitimate polls. The most recent installment of the bipartisan "Bullseye poll" that my firm conducts with a Democratic firm for National Journal's *Hotline* confirmed this. When asked to cite the most important issue this year, a sum total of 7 percent of women offered one of the following: pro-choice on abortion, gun control, campaign finance reform, gay rights, or tobacco.

Women barely mention these matters, but a casual observer to the 2000 presidential campaign might believe that these issues *dominate* female voting. When is the last time a television pundit breathlessly proclaimed that "a breakdown of family values" is higher on the list of concerns than abortion? Yet the numbers demonstrate this.

Survey statistics also make clear that women are motivated by the "SHE" cluster of issues, a term my firm coined in 1998 as a short-handed way to recall the policy priorities for women. "SHE" (Social Security, Health Care and Education) includes issues of primary concern for voting women but ones that do not lend themselves as easily to hyperbole such as, in the words of another political observer, "gays, guns, and God."

In addition to the tangible issues contemplated in the "SHE" orbit, women talk to pollsters about "the intangibles." These include leadership, character, and integrity. This is not a creation of the "vast right-wing conspiracy," but a painful concern to the legion of folks yearning for a restoration of honor and order to major institutions.

For years pollsters have asked Americans a variation of the question, "Do you think that the country is headed in the right direction, or have we seriously gotten off on the wrong track?" Often, the response reflected the state of the economy. As I listened to voters in focus groups across the country it became clear that an expansion of that inquiry was in order.

Focus groups are qualitative, not quantitative, in nature. They lack the methodological purity or scientific backing of a survey. Still, focus groups are illustrative in that they allow the participants to express freely how they feel about what they think, an important undertaking that is naturally limited in telephone polls where often the respondent is asked to answer "yes or no," "approve or disapprove," "support or oppose."

In focus groups, the conservative underpinnings of public opinion are often revealed. Careful attention to the cognitive processes, choice of language, and stated rationale revealed should compel more responsive, and more responsible, polling inquiries.

> **To many Americans, frankly, "tax" is still a four-letter word, frequently appearing in polling data as a chief concern for men and women, although infrequently mentioned in reports about voter anger or motivation, where again, abortion remains peerless.**

To this end, several years ago we began to separate the classic "right direction/wrong track" query, and with startling results. First, we would ask, "Thinking specifically about the economy for a moment, do you think that the economy in this country is heading in the right direction, or has it seriously gotten off on the wrong track?" Recently, those numbers have averaged around 68 percent right direction; 22 percent wrong track.

The very next question repeats the phraseology but changes topics. "Now, putting aside the economy for a moment, and focusing on the morals and standards of the country, in your opinion, are we headed in the right direction, or have we seriously gotten off on wrong track?" Amazingly, the numbers flip, with two-thirds of those surveyed saying "wrong track."

This figure has been especially high among women since we began asking the question two years ago.

It makes sense that if Americans have a bifurcated approach to some of these issues, so, too, must the polling inquiries that aim to uncover their opinions.

The shift away from womb-based politics and the drift toward cultural conservatism for many women is manifested at the ballot box. For all of the hysterical predictions about gender "canyons" and "abysses," actual election results suggest that women are more consistent and more conservative as voters than has been reported.

Sixty-three percent of women voted for Richard Nixon for reelection in 1972. A majority of women (55 percent) voted for Reagan-Bush in 1984, despite the Democrats' nomination of a woman (Geraldine Ferraro) for vice president. A majority of women, 51 percent, voted for Bush-Quayle in 1988, something that Clinton-Gore did not accomplish four years later. History may show that women have helped Bill Clinton do a number of things, but get elected may not have been chief among them.

Indeed, women are pro-incumbents. Women stick with what they know, and in the absence of a compelling reason, they avoid rocking the boat politically.

True, a slim majority of women have favored Democratic candidates in congressional elections, but strong pluralities have consistently pulled the GOP lever as well. In the ten congressional elections held between 1980 and 1998, the percentage of women voting successively for the Republican candidate has been a flat line since 1980: 46 percent, 42 percent, 46 percent, 46 percent, 43 percent, 46 percent, 45, 47, 45, 47. Men, over that same time, have more dramatically shifted their allegiances, with their preferences for congressional Republicans resembling a cardiogram for an angioplasty patient: 51, 45, 52, 49, 48, 49, 48, 58, 56, 54. For the fourth consecutive time, and with women accounting for more than one-half of the total vote, a Republican-led Congress and a majority of GOP governorships are about to be elected.

The real "gender gap" exists not so much among men and women as it does among women and women. One can chart differences in female voting behavior and political attitudes according to age and race/ethnicity or marital status, children living at home, and living parents.

The most remarkable feature of the "gender gap" in this year's election is Al Gore's trouble in attracting men. Many polls show Gore losing men by double digits to George W. Bush. If the way to a man's heart is through his stomach, then the way to a man's vote is through his pocketbook. And men, by and large, view the given conservative candidate as protective of their assets and the free market system generally. To many Americans, "tax" is still a four-letter word, frequently appearing in polling data as a chief concern for men and women, although infrequently mentioned in reports about voter anger or motivation where, again, abortion remains peerless.

Does a gender gap exist? Yes. But does the gender gap exist in life? Yes! Ladies and gentlemen, I have a news flash: men and women are different! We have different hardware and different software. We relate to issues differently, we respond differently to external stimuli, to things that we see, that we read. I am not surprised that these differences manifest themselves at the ballot box. What is confounding is the way the same androgynous Left that tries to blur gender differences on everything from parenting to "equal rights," insists on underscoring these differences through talk of a "gender gap."

The real "gender gap" exists not so much among men and women as it does among women and women. Rather than meld together the 100 million eligible female voters into an indistinguishable mass, it is wise to examine the *intra-gender gaps* among different groups of women.

One can chart differences in female voting behavior and political attitudes according to their immutable characteristics, like age and race/ethnicity or their choices and circumstances, such as marital status, children living at home, living parents, household income, property or portfolio ownership, frequency of religious participation, and geography.

To demonstrate, black women vote Democratic nearly 90 percent of the time. Unmarried women tend to identify with Democratic rhetoric about "security" and "inclusiveness." These women are more likely to agree that Uncle Sam should help provide and protect them. This can be true of younger unmarried women who are imprisoned by groupthink on our college campuses and older, widowed women who rely upon Social Security, Medicare or Medicaid and veterans' benefits.

The natural stations of life, including the three magic M's—"marriage, mortgage and munchkins"—move women toward a more conservative philosophy. A fourth "M," mutual funds, is emerging as well, as a majority of women now are investors, either directly in the stock market or indirectly through 401(k) or pension plans.

> **The natural stations of life, including the three magic M's—"marriage, mortgage and munchkins"—move women toward a more conservative philosophy.**

The so-called "Soccer Mom" from the 1996 elections has just retired her cleats. "Mutual Fund Momma" is the woman to court this year.

Another group of "women to watch" is the "sandwich generation." With women deferring child rearing until they are older, and with people living longer, some 28 percent of likely voters include women who have both children living at home and parents still living. These women put themselves third on their "to-do" lists, focusing on issues as diverse as prescription drugs and school choice, but with little concern—or time—for abortion politics.

Unfortunately, the proliferation of sloppy polling has helped to cement the status of abortion and its offspring, the gender gap, as prime political fodder. The obscene obsession with polling in our political culture has engendered overly narrow and simplistic questions, a presumption of knowledge among those being surveyed, instant moment-by-moment polls, the junk science of Internet polls, and ultimately, a confusion of coincidence and causation.

The fixation with the "horserace" or head-to-head ballot, feeds this beast. The near-constant question posed by media polls of "Gore or Bush" focuses on who *will* win, rather than who *should* win. The media's duty is to inform an electorate, not predict its behavior, which has a perverse effect on creating or molding that behavior.

The most popular way to poll abortion politics, "Are you pro-life or pro-choice?" is inadequate, if not unethical. Abortion is the one issue that combines religion, morality, science, medicine, law, politics, and gender. Fuller discussions with Americans have revealed that Americans are increasingly troubled with committing to a position on abortion unless they know the other "circumstances" ("Was she raped?" "How far along is the pregnancy?").

In our polls, we probe abortion on a six-point scale that allows for the gradation in viewpoints that obviously exist. The question is phrased: "Please tell me which of the following comes closest to your view on abortion (1) Abortion should be prohibited under all circumstances; (2) Abortion should be allowed, but only to save the life of the mother; (3) Abortion should be allowed, but only to save the life of the mother, or in cases of rape or incest; (4) Abortion should be allowed for any reason, but not past the first trimester or first three months of a woman's pregnancy; (5) Abortion should be allowed for any reason, but not past the first six months, or second trimester of a woman's pregnancy; and finally (6) Abortion should be allowed for any reason, at any time, during a woman's pregnancy?"

A majority of women agree with one of the first three statements, which represent the range of what has been accepted as pro-life positions. Add to that the fourth position—those who would not allow abortion after the first trimester—and two-thirds of women's opinions on abortion are accounted for. Only 14 percent of the country agrees with the final position, which is essentially the (Bill)Clinton-(Hillary)Clinton-Gore gospel of "abortion anytime, anywhere, anyone."

Politically, men *and* women are more conscious of issues than gender. The difference on issues is often one of intensity, not agreement. Bulging majorities of women may politely nod their head when presented with a pleasant-sounding concept, e.g., "campaign finance reform," "gun control," "choice," but differ on the relative importance of that concept to them or their vote (is there really a contest between lower taxes and campaign finance reform?) or the specific policies they would choose to address these issues (e.g., school choice or teacher tenure). The proliferation of shoddy polling has come at a particular dicey time in American history. With game shows *and* gamely showiness in vogue, everyone wants to sound and seem smart about everything. Our instantaneous lifestyle, from Botox lunches to e-mail "conversations," has created an expectation that anything worth hearing or having should be obtained in seven seconds or less.

Most Americans want to be informed, but not necessarily educated, on issues. We favor "news-you-can-use" material. This contributes to the primacy of polling in that a snappy sound bite or statistic can be conveyed succinctly and memorably. The poll today is the entire story. It is the subject. It is the predicate. It is the headline. It is the byline. It is a disgrace.

Most poll questions simply ask people to respond to feel-good phraseology without probing their underlying ideology. This invites confusion between causation and coincidence and proves that that which is meaningless is open to many interpretations of its meaning.

For all the fluctuations in the polls, one thing is really true one month before this year's election. Some 9 percent of likely voters remain firmly undecided, playing wait-and-see. These "uncommitted" faithful are mostly women, who traditionally reserve final judgment until closer to Election Day. Many of these women make a race difficult to predict. Eventually, this race will depend upon the last two or three things that were impressed upon, believed to be true, or heard by these voters.

The ultimate success of conservatives in appreciating, not agonizing over, the gender gap, and in responding effectively to the nuances among men and women, will center in how the proverbial debate is cast.

If the debate is political, that is, "Right versus Left," conservatives are disadvantaged. Liberal Democrats have more clever sound bites, better care tactics, and bigger goodies to give away.

If the debate is philosophical, that is, "Right versus Wrong," conservatives benefit. This framework demands application of common sense, and a return to the brand of core values and order that form the basis of free will and personal responsibility. ■

Another centrist Clinton judge, Harold Baer Jr., ruled that there was no "probable cause" to arrest suspects who flee at the sight of police officers while loading bags into the trunk of a car late at night in a high drug-trafficking area.

—Ann Coulter

DEMOCRATS ADVICE TO BUSH:

Keep Your Judges Off My Judiciary!

BY ANN COULTER
WASHINGTON, D.C., JUNE 5, 2000
EXCERPTS FROM A SPEECH AT THE CONSERVATIVE WOMEN'S NETWORK

LET ME START BY SAYING—I love speaking on college campuses. The environments are so hegemonically left-wing that any students who bring me to speak are invariably the rebels. They're always bright, politically active, and appear to wake up every morning thinking: What can I do today to annoy liberals? Apparently, bringing me to speak is one of the popular options.

Politics has gotten rather boring of late—what with the president not being a felon. So I thought I'd cheer you up by telling you we can look forward to World War III when Bush announces his first Supreme Court nominee.

The *New York Times* has been nostalgically reminiscing about Clinton's—quote—"centrist judicial choices" and

denouncing the wild-eyed ideologues it assumes will be favored by Bush. Indeed, the entire Rainbow Coalition is on red alert in anticipation of George

ANN COULTER is an attorney specializing in constitutional law. She is a nationally syndicated columnist and author *of Slander: Liberal Lies About the American Right.* An expert on legal and political issues she appears frequently on television. Coulter lives in New York City.

Bush appointing judges who agree with him, rather than them.

Ralph G. Neas, president of People For the American Way, said, "There is more at stake in these nominations than ever before in our history." (Can you imagine the hue and cry if an actually patriotic organization called itself that?)

Evidently, there aren't a lot of Americans who believe in "the American Way," otherwise liberals wouldn't have to demand federal judges who invent ludicrous "constitutional rights" that the American people would never vote for.

Neas, along with the ACLU, the ABA, La Raza, and—the most vicious left-wing propaganda machine of all—the media, insist their Soviet agitprop against strict constructionists has nothing whatsoever to do with politics. No. They say they evaluate judges solely on the basis of their respect for the Constitution. As Neas put it: "The Senate owes its first allegiance to the American people and to the Constitution."

By "Constitution" he means every crackpot "right" liberals have been able to sneak into Supreme Court opinions in the last fifty years. And there are lots of them: rights for killers, pornographers, stinky homeless people, transsexuals, and nonsmokers. The "Constitution" is oddly silent, however, on the rights of babies, crime victims, law-abiding citizens, and property-owners.

But liberals can't admit that what they mean by "constitutional rights" is a collection of ideological victories completely unconnected to the language of the Constitution. Otherwise the American people would be against (drumroll): "the American Way."

SO LIBERALS SPEAK IN CODE:

- "Constitutional rights" = the entire ideological agenda of the ACLU
- "Privacy rights" = sticking a fork in a baby's head
- "Ideologues" = people who don't see anything allowing the destruction of fetus's brains in the Constitution
- "Moderates" = people who believe the Constitution strictly prohibits punishing criminals
- "Centrist" = certifiably insane.

> **The entire Rainbow Coalition is on red alert in anticipation of George Bush appointing judges who agree with him, rather than them.**

Now *New York Times* editorials will make sense to you.

"Centrist" law professor Cass Sunstein of the University of Chicago has written an hysterical jeremiad in the *New York Times* about the danger of conservative judges "who would interpret the Constitution...in a way that promotes [their] agenda."

But the only "agenda" strict constructionists have is to return to a constitutional democracy so we can live in freedom and decide issues for ourselves.

Hallucinating history, just like the liberals' pet judges hallucinate "constitutional rights," Sunstein complained about the Republican juggernaut stopping all the "centrists" nominated to the federal bench by Clinton.

Sunstein says Republicans "did whatever they could to block Mr. Clinton's judicial nominees. Meanwhile, Democratic senators unwilling to base rejection of nominees on political disagreements, have usually deferred to Republican presidents."

Maybe they just hated Clarence Thomas because he was black. Still, Sunstein insists, Democrats have been "remarkably passive."

One more definition:

"Passive" = willing to start World War III.

Let's review the record on Clinton's "centrist" judges.

One of Clinton's "centrist" choices, Judge H. Lee Sarokin, found that a homeless man had a constitutional right to stink up libraries and frighten patrons with his obsessive staring. The "offensive odor" standard at the library violated the First Amendment apparently because it was a library and there are books in a library, which contain speech, which is protected by the First Amendment.

The No-Stinking-the-Place-Up rule also violated "substantive due process" (which doesn't exist) because the odor rule was a "reader-based restriction." And it violated the equal protection clause (which does exist) because of the "disparate impact" the rule had on people who refuse to bathe.

In a rousing summary that will go down in history with Justice Holmes's "three generations of imbeciles are enough," Judge Sarokin wrote that instead of hoping to "shield our eyes and ears from the homeless...we should revoke their condition, not their library cards."

The Senate confirmed Sarokin's appointment to the Third Circuit, 63-35, on October 4, 1994. A few years later, Sarokin petulantly retired when the court unaccountably refused to let him sit in California on the opposite side of the country from the Third Circuit, which covers New Jersey, Pennsylvania, and Delaware.

Another centrist Clinton judge, Harold Baer Jr., received nationwide attention a few years ago for his ruling that there was no "probable cause" to arrest suspects who flee at the sight of police officers while loading bags into the trunk of a car late at night in a high drug-trafficking area. Baer explained that, in that neighborhood, the police are viewed as "corrupt, abusive and violent." Consequently, it was perfectly rational to run at the sight of them.

In addition to any vague feelings of ill-will the defendants might have harbored toward law enforcement, they evidently also had reason to flee that particular night on account of the 80 pounds of cocaine in their possession.

This, Judge Baer excluded from evidence. He later reversed himself—but only because it was a presidential election year and he was about to become the next Willie Horton.

The Republican juggernaut against Clinton's judicial nominees led to a unanimous Senate confirmation for Judge Baer who was appointed to the District Court for the Southern District of New York on August 9, 1994.

On the basis of her habit of apologizing to criminals during sentencing, District Court Judge Sonia Sotomayor had earned wide acclaim as a "centrist" long before Clinton elevated her to a federal appeals court. While sentencing one drug-dealer, she said: "[W]e all understand that you were in part a victim of the economic necessities of our society; unfortunately there are laws that I must impose."

She told another convicted drug trafficker: "It is no comfort to you for me to say that I am deeply, personally sorry about the sentence that I must impose, because the law requires me to do so. The only statement I can make is this is one more example of an abomination being committed before our sight. You do not deserve this, sir."

It may have been the "sir" that kept it from being unanimous. Sotomayor was confirmed to the Second Circuit Court of Appeals in a 68-28 vote.

Judge Diane Wood, centrist judge put on the U.S. Court of Appeals for the Seventh Circuit by Clinton, found that failure to provide a prisoner with a smoke-free environment constituted cruel and unusual punishment. Another centrist Clinton choice, Judge Robert Henry, held that it was cruel and unusual punishment for the state to deny sex change hormone treatment for a transsexual prisoner. Every time you hear the words "centrist," "moderate," "mainstream," just remember: This is what they mean. ■

CURRENT READINESS PROBLEMS CAUSED BY CLINTON-ERA POLICIES WILL AFFECT PRESIDENT BUSH'S ABILITY TO FIGHT THE WAR WE ARE WAGING.

—ELAINE DONNELLY

BILL CLINTON'S MILITARY:
Under New Management

BY ELAINE DONNELLY
WASHINGTON, D.C., MARCH 8, 2002
EXCERPTS FROM A SPEECH AT THE CONSERVATIVE WOMEN'S NETWORK

I AM DELIGHTED TO BE HERE. Michelle Easton—the Conservative Women's Network—and I have been working for a long time to foster leadership among women. This is most important in respect to the military.

Last October, I had the privilege of speaking at another wonderful organization, the Independent Women's Forum, to honor one of their founders, the late Barbara Olson, who was killed by terrorists when her plane crashed into the Pentagon on September 11. Barbara was a true woman warrior. In the final terrifying moments of her life, she called her husband, Ted Olson, and asked, "What should I tell the pilot to do?" As the War on Terrorism continues, patriotic women need to consider: "What should we tell the president to do?"

That day changed the life of the nation—our lives—forever.

Today America is engaged in a real War on Terrorism. After September 11th, we can no longer afford to think of the military as just another equal

ELAINE DONNELLY is founder and president of the Center for Military Readiness, an independent public policy organization that specializes in military personnel issues. She has served on the Defense Advisory Committee on Women in the Services (DACOWITS), and the 1992 Presidential Commission on Women in the Armed Forces.

opportunity employer, just another career opportunity. The issues that I deal with are not women's issues, but issues of national defense that involve women.

For the last eight years, Pentagon feminists have tried to use the military for purposes of social engineering. They have advocated a politically correct, "ungendered" military, to use their term. They have demanded that Pentagon officials do certain things in order to prove the feminist theory that men and women are interchangeable in all military occupations, including close combat.

I place no blame on military women for what's happened in the last eight years. They have had no more say about feminist policies than the men have. The views of enlisted women are routinely trampled upon by a few select officers and civilian Pentagon feminists who claim to speak for all women.

I support women in the military. I do not support their assignment to close combat units. The definition is important because "close combat" means directly engaging the enemy on land, sea, or in the air. On the land are Special Forces and infantry units that we have seen fighting in Afghanistan. On the sea are submarines. In the air, it's fighter aircraft and special operations helicopters. These are combat units that feminists in the Pentagon look upon as "career opportunities" for women.

So how do you sort this all out? In 1992, during the first Bush administration, I served on the Presidential Commission on the Assignment of Women in the Armed Forces with several distinguished people, including some liberals. The biggest debates we had were over a very simple principle: Equal opportunity in the military is important; but if there is a conflict between career considerations and military necessity, the needs of the military *must* come first.

Simple? Yes, but controversial. Those who advocated women in land combat insisted that equal opportunity should come first. For the last eight years, Pentagon feminists and their allies have been promoting "career opportunities" for women as their highest priority, even at the expense of readiness.

After September 11th, we can no longer afford to think of the military as just another equal opportunity employer.

In the end, the presidential commission came out against women in land and aviation combat, and for a host of recommendations involving family issues and high training standards. Everybody was surprised, since many observers expected the commission to be a rubber stamp for the liberal position. Instead, several women involved in public policy didn't wait for somebody to tell them what to do. Drawing upon their own intelligence, common sense, and the advice of military experts, a narrow majority voted against women in combat.

The day we voted, however, was November 4, 1992—the day George Bush Sr. lost the election and Bill Clinton took over. Virtually all of our recommendations were not only ignored, the Clinton Defense Department did exactly the opposite.

Scores of feminists were appointed to the Defense Department policy-making positions, and the Defense

Advisory Committee on Women in the Services. DACOW-
ITS, composed primarily of civilian women with virtually no
knowledge of military affairs, is the power base for Pentagon
feminists. They have the protocol status of three-star generals,
and admirals, which matters. They are very skilled at intimi-
dating or manipulating male military leaders, both uniformed
and civilian. And they never stop pushing their agenda, step
by incremental step.

Michelle Easton, among other women leaders, joined me at a
recent news conference at which we called on the president to
abolish the DACOWITS. This, I'm happy to report, was wel-
comed by many at the Pentagon and had a significant impact.

SOME PEOPLE THINK THAT SINCE BILL CLINTON is no longer in
office, the problems he caused will be automatically solved.
Unfortunately, that is not the case.

The armed forces are a third to a half smaller now than during Desert Storm. There is also a high pregnancy rate in the
military, and few if any replacements for women who cannot
be deployed. We can no longer afford to retain gender quotas
for military personnel who are less strong, less versatile, and
more likely to leave early. In support units people can be
moved around more easily, but today there are no extra people
to move around.

Current readiness problems caused by Clinton-era policies
will affect President Bush's ability to fight the war we are waging. This is because the armed forces face two major problems:

The consequences of drastic budget cuts over many years, and readiness problems caused by years of demoralizing social engineering. On the first point:

> For the last eight years, Pentagon feminists and their allies have been promoting "career opportunities" for women as their highest priority, even at the expense of readiness.

When the carrier *Theodore Roosevelt* departed from Norfolk right after the September attack on America, it was fully prepared for its mission. The planes had engines, spare parts, sufficient fuel, and impressive weapons to help them accomplish their dangerous missions. But when that carrier returns, many of the planes will be taken to a hanger and their engines will be cannibalized for spare parts, because many of the aircraft are not being manufactured anymore.

On September 10, the day before the terrorists attacked America, this headline appeared in *Navy Times*: "Duct Tape Aviation: How Old Planes and Parts Shortages are Running Aircraft and Sailors Ragged." Maintenance problems caused by budget cuts have been going on for a long time. Just before the September attacks, an F-14 training squadron was reported to have only ten of thirty-five aircraft capable of flying. This is frightening.

Then there was a *Navy Times* cover story last year: "Band-Aid Navy: How Shortages Are Burning Out Sailors and Wearing Out the Fleet." It's the kind of thing that can go on only for so long without drastic consequences.

Consider the status of the carrier *John F. Kennedy*. Another *Navy Times* headline put it succinctly: "CV-67, Where Are You?" CV-67 is the carrier *Kennedy*, which was late going to the theater of war to replace the *Roosevelt*. When the *Roosevelt* finally returns, it will be reported as the longest deployment on record.

Why was the *Kennedy* late? Because the readiness inspection was a dismal failure. The elevators that take the aircraft up on deck were not working; the catapults were not functioning reliably; and there were all kinds of electrical problems. The *Kennedy* wasn't ready, even though millions of dollars had been spent on emergency repairs.

Shortly after the *Kennedy* finally deployed, a tragedy occurred. One of the aircraft crashed on take-off, possibly because of a malfunctioning catapult. One pilot perished.

What should President Bush do about military readiness? The first thing, which I think he's already done, is to call in his generals and admirals and insist that officers at all levels be absolutely candid about the condition of the military. In the Clinton years, one of the major problems was that the chairman of the Joint Chiefs and other high-level officers told Congress that everything was just fine—the politically correct response. Then, just before the election, surprise, they admitted that our readiness problems were severe and getting worse.

In addition, the armed forces have been suffering from what has been loaded on by social engineers in the Pentagon. One of these ideologues was a woman by the name of Sara Lister, an assistant secretary of the army who caused a huge controversy when she called the marines "extremist."

The commandant of the Marine Corps was infuriated by her insulting remark, defenders of the corps made speeches on the floor of Congress, and Sara Lister was forced to resign within forty-eight hours. But the unrealistic social policies that Lister imposed on the army, such as co-ed basic training, remained in force, and led to sexual misconduct scandals at Aberdeen Proving Grounds and basic training facilities around the country. Lister was an advocate of the "ungendered military."

Again, I'm not talking about career opportunities for women to serve our country. I'm talking about "social fiction" that denies reality. Social fiction is like science fiction; it looks real but it's not.

Social fiction tells you that men and women are interchangeable in all military roles, including land combat; that there are no dramatic differences in physical strength between the sexes; and to the extent that there are, they simply don't matter. It is possible to obscure the effect of physical strength differences by means of "gender norming," which gives credit to women for equal *effort*, which is not the same as equal *results*. So if a woman cannot run as fast or as far as a man, that's okay. She gets an "A" for achievements that would earn a "D" for a man. The problem with that is there is no gender norming on the battlefield.

Another form of social fiction insists that sexuality doesn't matter. If there are disciplinary problems between men and women who are mutually attracted, sensitivity training will take care of it. Social fiction also suggests that the military is useful for purposes of social experimentation because, thanks to high technology, "we're not going to have to fight real wars anymore." This odd argument continues to pop up even today.

Bill Clinton's military had other major problems starting with the newly elected president's call to permit open homosexuality in the military. In 1993, Congress passed a law *excluding* homosexuals from the military and affirming the long-standing principle that homosexuality is incompatible with military service. But the Clinton administration just ignored the law. They wanted a "don't ask, don't tell" policy— a policy that Congress rejected—which said that homosexuality is "personal and private and *not* a bar to military service." Another bit of social fiction that contributes to widespread confusion to this day.

Clinton-era social policies encouraged sexual tensions and indiscipline, rather than discipline. After the Tailhook 1991 sexual misconduct uproar, male aviators were literally purged from the navy, even though many were found innocent of any wrongdoing. The real scandal was that women officers were also involved, but they were not punished. If those aviators had not been thrown out and their colleagues demoralized by the obvious injustice, they would be out there fighting our war today. Enormous recruiting and retention problems have followed from all forms of Clinton-era sexual misconduct in the ranks, followed by efforts to weaken disciplinary rules even more.

Before the election, I received quite a few messages from military people who said, I've got my retirement papers ready; I want to see who wins this election. And who gave Bush/Cheney the margin of victory? The military, and voters who support a strong national defense.

> **Current readiness problems caused by Clinton-era policies will affect President Bush's ability to fight the war we are waging.**

Today, some social engineering policies are being set aside. *Insight* magazine reported that in the aftermath of September 11, when the reserves were called up, the order was to include pregnant women reservists. Some Pentagon officials were astonished, but that indeed was the Clinton policy. The current undersecretary of defense for personnel and readiness, Dr. David Chu, however, rescinded the order. But an underlying readiness problem remains. Commanders in field units and ships will have to deploy shorthanded.

During the Gulf War, service women were found to be almost four times as nondeployable as the men, and female sailors were evacuated from navy ships for medical reasons, primarily pregnancy, at rates two-and-one-half times more than men.

These are realities. They can't be ignored because we have too few sailors to go around. Yet, undaunted by facts, the Pentagon feminists have been trying for years to impose these problems on submarines, where living quarters are far more restrictive, and evacuation problems far more severe than in the rest of the fleet.

The Department of Navy has pointed out that the atmosphere on a submarine is safe for adults but toxic for an unborn child. If a female sailor discovers she is pregnant, the captain can either go to the surface, compromising the mission of the sub, or continue to sail, knowingly risking the health of the unborn child. It's a tough, unfair decision to have to make. The British navy decided not to accept female submariners for that reason alone. And yet, when the DACOWITS committee was confronted with this information they were adamant: women's careers should be given the highest priority.

In the army, co-ed basic training aggravates disciplinary problems. Many basic trainers spend time keeping the guys and the girls apart—you know, like in high school. Most of the women involved in consensual sexual misconduct at Aberdeen were exploited by senior drill instructors. It was an all-too-common phenomenon that I like to call consexploitation—the same thing the commander-in-chief was involved in with Monica Lewinsky.

Early last year, we found out that the infantry school at Fort Benning is devoting seven of seventeen weeks to co-ed basic officer training. Never mind that women don't serve in the infantry. Some members of Congress wrote to the secretary of the army asking, how does this benefit the infantry soldiers? They're still waiting for an answer.

A new army land combat unit is being formed that you're going to hear a lot more about. It's the Interim Brigade Combat Teams, or IBCT. The IBCT Surveillance Troop will fight for intelligence on the ground. It means going into caves to find out where the bad guys are, it means putting your life at great risk.

Well, we found out last fall that the Surveillance Troop, the hottest thing going in the army, is training women. This is contrary to law and policy, but Pentagon feminists see this primarily as a "career opportunity."

The DACOWITS has also pushed for years to have women in special operations helicopters like the ones used in Somalia and featured in the film *Black Hawk Down*. Do you remember Michael Durant—a man whose battered face appeared on the cover of news magazines at the time? He was a special operation's helicopter pilot.

In April of last year, all of the DACOWITS members were Clinton members. This is because Clinton holdovers used the autopen of newly appointed Defense Secretary Donald Rumsfeld to ratify the selection of DACOWITS members chosen by his predecessor, William Cohen. This was done without informing Secretary Rumsfeld. DACOWITS is not only radical, it is insubordinate. That's reason alone to abolish the committee.

To sum up on the DACOWITS: I have a letter from a Special Forces soldier who had read that the DACOWITS was being abolished. He wrote, "Thank you, thank you, thank you." We cannot afford to let that soldier down.

It is encouraging that the old DACOWITS charter was allowed to expire, but the new one continues to place a great deal of emphasis on professional development, equal opportunity, and women's careers.

It is reassuring to see a defense team that is putting social fiction aside, and taking war seriously. They are not being sidetracked by politics, or wayward allies. We are now waging a war with Bill Clinton's military, but it's under new management. President Bush is not bound by the polls and doesn't care what other nations think. This president knows that our freedoms are at risk, and our way of life depends on a strong national defense. And what a difference it has made!

We need to support this president. And we need to help restore the strength and morale of the finest military in the world. ■

DO YOU REALIZE THAT THE LAWS IN OUR COUNTRY EXACT A MORE SEVERE PUNISHMENT FOR DESTROYING CONDOR EGGS THAN FOR DESTROYING ANOTHER HUMAN BEING?
—BECKY NORTON DUNLOP

CLEARING THE AIR

BY BECKY NORTON DUNLOP
WASHINGTON, D.C., JANUARY 12, 2001
EXCERPTS FROM A SPEECH AT THE CONSERVATIVE WOMEN'S NETWORK

AMERICA IS A GREAT COUNTRY because America is a free country, and America is a beautiful country partly because of Americans who not only espouse conservative philosophy, but also have been good conservationists throughout the years.

I've fought in conservative battles in a number of fields—education, federalism, welfare reform, private property, privatization, outdoor recreation, and the family. For most of these issues I managed task forces for Ed Meese, President Reagan's attorney general, who served as chairman of the president's Domestic Policy Council. It seemed apparent to me that conservative ideas were winning the hearts and minds of the American people. Then I spotted a new battle, a battle I considered vital to the country, and a battle we were not yet winning.

I joined Secretary Don Hodel's management team at the Department of the Interior the last two years of the Reagan administration and during the transition for President Bush. There I became even more convinced that the environment

BECKY NORTON DUNLOP is vice president of external relations at The Heritage Foundation. From 1994 to 1998 she served as secretary of natural resources in Virginia Governor George Allen's cabinet. She is the author of *Clearing the Air: How the People of Virginia Improved the State's Air and Water Despite the EPA* (see Heritage.org). She and her husband, George, live in Virginia.

was liberalism's last bastion of command and control in the American political system. That's not to say that conservatives have won and institutionalized victories in the other areas. But conservative ideas are making progress, because intellectually, the American people are on the conservative side in those areas.

But the environmental issues had been neglected by conservatives because we focused almost all of our attention on many of those other areas that seemed vastly more important to preserving our liberty. Increasingly, the environment became an area around which the command and control liberal establishment, the people who believe in collectivist government, began to gather. Those who are now active in the extremist environmental movement are those who believe that all power should be centralized in Washington, D.C., in the federal government. They do not trust people, they do not trust governors, they do not trust state legislators, and they certainly do not trust the private sector. They want to have all power collected and dispensed by the federal government; that is, to their way of thinking, by themselves and their friends and political allies.

Then there are those who believe in a socialist form of government, that government should own the land, that the private sector will damage the land and that capitalism is synonymous with environmental exploitation and degradation. That group of people also makes up a major part of the radical environmental movement of today.

Finally, there are the people who have a religious conviction about the environment. Some people actually think that human beings, you and me, are not valuable, at least not as valuable as rocks and trees and other critters. Do you realize that the laws in our country exact a more severe punishment for destroying condor eggs than for destroying another human being? And government is aggressive about this enforcement.

I became even more convinced that the environment was liberalism's last bastion of command and control in the American political system.

These are basically the three groups that make up the environmental extremists—the politicized "party of government" partisans, the socialists, and the pantheists—and they have been very, very successful. For, through the earnest efforts of their handmaidens in the national news media, they have essentially captured the hearts and minds of the American people. But those of us who believe strongly that private property rights are a core element of the American system of liberty have begun to fight back.

We have learned many lessons in our conservation and environmental stewardship practices, all of which have been advanced by education and science. Yet these two areas are where the liberals really fall down on the job. They're not interested in providing citizens with more scientific education, which is why we have had some challenges.

After serving with Don Hodel, a great mentor, I was associated with Citizens for a Sound Economy which was starting to educate its members on the environmental issue. Those of you who think about this issue will understand that a growing economy and an improving environment go hand in hand— *not* something you will hear the "Green" activists say. While helping with the Citizens for a Sound Economy project, I also began supporting the National Wilderness Institute, an environmental organization that acts on sound scientific principles, something completely foreign to such officials as Secretary Bruce Babbitt, Al Gore, and others who rely on pseudo-science and fear-mongering as the basis for their brand of environmental activism. Do you remember when we had the Alar scare in this country? Whom did the liberal leaders in Congress bring in to testify? Meryl Streep, the actress. A scientist? I don't think so; how about pseudo-scientist?

The liberals' objective in the Alar scare was to frighten our people, every mom and every child in America; and they also succeeded in destroying the livelihoods of hundreds of families involved in the apple industry—all of this based on no scientific evidence. And we all know that what our moms used to tell us—"an apple a day keeps the doctor away"—was good advice, and was based on good science.

I wrote my book, *Clearing the Air*, after serving four years with Governor George Allen of Virginia as his cabinet secretary for Natural Resources. During that time the battle was engaged, conservatives were determined to demonstrate that our philosophy was good for the environment and good for the people.

When George Allen had a press conference to announce me

as his natural resources secretary, the
Washington Post reporter, whom I didn't
know but assumed was going at least to
give us a fair chance, said, "How old are
you, Becky?" I hadn't heard him ask that
of any of the men. And I said, "Well, a
gentleman never asks that question of a
lady." (I thought, "A soft answer turneth
away wrath.") "Well, I'm not a gentleman," he retorted.

> Those who are now active in the extremist environmental movement are those who believe that all power should be centralized in Washington, D.C., in the federal government.

The next question the press asked was,
"Is Becky a payoff for the Christian Right?" I make no bones
about the fact that I'm a committed Christian. In my state-
ment accepting my position, I not only thanked all the people,
I thanked God, the Creator of our natural resources. But
George Allen did not let me answer that question. He said,
"Becky Norton Dunlop is a payoff for the citizens of Virginia."

Let me tell you, when you get that kind of support right off
the bat, you're loyal. For four years, my office was under constant attack from the liberal environmentalists, and George
Allen never wavered in his support.

Some of the stories I tell in the book are about our battles
with the federal Environmental Protection Agency. I'm certain
that the Allen administration was not one of the favorites of
Carol Browner, Clinton's head of the EPA. And I had serious
disagreements with folks I thought were wrong or far too liberal on issues with which we were dealing. But I was always civil

and I think that is an important attribute for success. I had an open door policy, through which environmentalists were invited whenever they wanted to visit with me. Their approach was slightly different. About two months after I took office, a group of environmental activists got together in a private meeting in Northern Virginia to discuss how they were going to deal with the Allen administration. You see, we were nice and civil, saying to them, "We will invite you to participate in all our meetings. You just won't be the only ones invited and you won't be running the show." There could be no legitimate complaint about being excluded, because they were not. But all this notwithstanding, they announced to the press that they were never invited to meetings. That's exactly their style of operation.

To effectively deal with such people and their agenda, one must operate from a principled position. So, let me give you a few principles that guided me. These principles were not kept secret but were openly announced and discussed for four years. I wrote articles about them and referred to them in every speech I gave.

MY NUMBER ONE: People are our most important and valuable natural resource. People live on this planet and should be allowed to use its natural resources. We must also conserve and seek to enhance them. We will educate our people and use good science, but it's the people themselves who will come up with solutions for every environmental challenge we face.

The Allen position was that we were not going to engage in mandates, funded or unfunded, and we were not going to tell people how to live their lives. We were going to involve them and when we found environmental problems, were going to help them develop solutions.

NUMBER TWO: Renewable natural resources are resilient and dynamic and respond positively to wise management. We need to have management, no question about it, but resources *are* dynamic and resilient.

I like to use the Chesapeake Bay in Virginia as an example. Fifteen years ago, people didn't want to go out into the Chesapeake Bay because it was in such bad shape. Today, the bay is crowded on the weekends. The same goes for the Potomac River and the Anacostia River, right here in Washington, D.C. And then there's the Cuyahoga River in Ohio, which actually caught fire twenty years ago. Today, the most expensive real estate in northern Ohio is on the banks of the Cuyahoga River.

NUMBER THREE: If we apply wise management, we improve our natural resources. How does America have the wherewithal to improve natural resources? From a growing economy! People have money, they have jobs, and their families are cared for. They look around and see what else they can improve.

The most promising new opportunities for environmental improvements lie in extending the protection of private property and unleashing the creative powers of the free market. It's been proven time and time again throughout history and around the world.

NUMBER FOUR: Make real efforts to reduce, control, and remediate pollution to achieve real environmental benefits. How many environmental groups do you know that raise money and with that money hold meetings? And has anything from those meetings really improved the environment? No, it just does not happen.

Liberal extremists are not interested in improving the environment. Because what happens when things get better? Bureaucracy is reduced in size. You would think after eight years of the Clinton-Gore-Browner administration with its heavy environmental focus that someone, any one of them, would be pointing to a success. Instead, every speech they give is about how many environmental problems we have. What have they been doing? They've been having meetings.

NUMBER FIVE: The learning curve is green. What do I mean? Every day, we learn something new and our new information and new technology allow us to use less of a given natural resource. We use less natural resources to make Coca-Cola cans because we have new technologies. Our cars get better mileage. As for the timber in our forests, we get more and more board feet from a tree and we use every part of that tree. The list goes on and on.

NUMBER SIX: Management of natural resources should be conducted on a site and case-by-case basis. It's logical. The things that affect air quality in Washington, D.C., are different from the things that affect air quality in Phoenix, Arizona.

NUMBER SEVEN: Science should be employed as a tool to guide public policy. But it was not always so in Carol Browner's EPA. We could give you example after example after example of where her decisions were based on political science, not sound science.

How many of you were in town when we had the pfisteria scare? You would have thought that the world was coming to an end because of pfisteria. And EPA and the environmental extremists were so eager; they wanted to find pfisteria in Virginia and they couldn't, but I'll tell you, they sure were out there looking. Because they had pfisteria in the waters of Maryland— where, by the way, Parris Glendening, Mr. Green, is the governor. But in Virginia, we had managed our natural resources and we had worked with our businesses on environmental quality and we did not have the same problems that they had.

The reason, incidentally, could have nothing to do with managing resources or working with businesses. It could be entirely a natural phenomenon. There are some things mankind can't control, so one looks for ways to manage natural resources based on the best available sound science.

NUMBER EIGHT: The final conservative environmental principle—which you might suspect coming from me—is that environmental policies that emanate from liberty are the most successful. Where do people in the world turn today for solutions? Our country. We have technology, we're on the cutting edge, we're always looking for new and better ways to improve our quality of life. Because we have a free enterprise system, we have entrepreneurs who are always looking for solutions for environmental challenges. We're Americans!

These principles stood us in good stead during George Allen's governorship in Virginia. The quality and condition of the environment improved significantly, and the economic success and "pursuit of happiness" that our citizens enjoyed had never been greater or more widespread.

Conservatives learned that we can win the hearts and minds of the people on environmental issues when we demonstrate that we are eager and able to apply our conservative principles to improving the quality and condition of the resources important to environmental quality.

This is a lesson that conservatives need to appreciate in the months and years ahead. ■

These education-ists wanted nothing less than a total monopoly over the formal intellectual training of children, and they almost got it.

—MICHELLE EASTON

EDUCATION IN AMERICA TODAY

BY MICHELLE EASTON
WASHINGTON, D.C., SEPTEMBER 13, 2002
EXCERPTS FROM A SPEECH AT THE CONSERVATIVE WOMEN'S NETWORK

ON FEBRUARY 20 OF THIS YEAR, the U.S. Supreme Court heard oral arguments on *Taylor vs. Simmons-Harris,* commonly called the Cleveland voucher case. A small African-American child, one of hundreds who rallied before the Supreme Court that day, held a sign that best expressed the argument before the Court: *"Who died and left the government my parents?"*

Freedom-loving Americans have high hopes that this will be a landmark decision—more sweeping than *Pierce vs. Society of Sisters* in 1925 and *Brown vs. Board of Education* in 1954; that the Court will unequivocally restore to families the right to determine the education of their children, the right that has been systematically stolen over the past 150 years.

The Founding Fathers had it right with the Tenth Amendment: "The powers not delegated to the United States by the Constitution, nor prohibited by it to the states, are reserved to the states respectively, or to the people."

Education was a power initially del-

MICHELLE EASTON is president and founder of the Clare Boothe Luce Policy Institute. She served 12 years in the administrations of President Reagan and President Bush and four years on the Virginia State Board of Education, two years as president. She lives in Virginia with her husband and three sons.

egated to the people. Thomas Jefferson introduced a proposal in the Virginia state legislature in 1779 to establish three years of tax-supported elementary schooling, but the proposal failed. For the first 175 years, parents shaped the education of their children largely free of government influence.

Then, in 1826, Massachusetts enacted a law requiring towns to establish school committees, organize schools under a single authority, and raise taxes for their support. And power struggles between parents and educationists began. An article in the *Massachusetts Teacher* in 1851 complained, "In too many instances the parents are unfit guardians of their own children...the children must be gathered up and forced into school."

At about the same time that the National Education Association was formed, 1857, states began enacting compulsory public school attendance laws—a process that was completed by 1918. Indeed, "Throughout the second half of the nineteenth century," writes historian Andrew Coulson, "education reformers, bureaucrats, and teachers' organizations pushed to increase their powers" over children and schooling. The Wisconsin Teachers' Association went so far as to assert that "children are the property of the state," an opinion that echoed many sister groups.

These educationists wanted nothing less than a total monopoly over the formal intellectual training of children, and they almost got it. Oregon revised its compulsory school law to make it illegal to send a child to a nonpublic school; however, in 1925 (*Pierce vs. Society of Sisters*), the Court struck down Oregon's law, writing:

> The fundamental theory upon which all governments in the Union repose excludes any general power of the State to standardize its children by forcing them to accept instruction from public teachers only. The child is not the mere creature of the State; those who nurture him and direct his destiny have the right, coupled with the high duty, to recognize and prepare him for additional obligation.

Recognizing that a virtual monopoly could still be achieved, NEA encouraged its members in 1932 to become societal change agents, and "influence the social attitudes, ideals, and behavior of the coming generation.

Unrepentant, and recognizing that a virtual monopoly could still be achieved, NEA encouraged its members in 1932 to become societal change agents, to "fashion the curriculum and procedures of the school" and "influence the social attitudes, ideals, and behavior of the coming generation."

They have never looked back.

■ The NEA was the driving force behind the creation of the federal Department of Education in 1979, one giant step toward government centralization of power and influence in education.

For a total of seven years straddling the eighties and nineties, I was an "ed fed," starting with work for President Reagan at the federal Department of Education in 1981 in an attempt to carry out his campaign pledge to abolish the department, which was justified then and now. Even the *Washington Post*, by no means a Reagan ally, acknowledged in a 1994 editorial: "There is a lot right about considering whether certain Cabinet departments deserve to be abolished. America's schools are not noticeably better because a Department of Education was created."

■ The NEA and its state affiliates have been the strongest opponents of academic standards, student testing, and public school accountability.

Nearly twenty years ago President Reagan's secretary of education Bill Bennett called the NEA union the most powerful obstacle to improving education in America. He's right. From its 1918 "Cardinal Principles" to the 1940s "Life Adjustment" curriculum and the 1960s "open schooling," the NEA has consistently shown a disdain for teaching traditional academic subjects such as English, math, and history, and a propensity for anti-intellectual curricula on the order of "Satisfactory Social Relationships," "Adjustment to Occupation," and "Development of Meaning for Life."

Luce Policy Institute Education Director Lil Tuttle and I witnessed this first hand in the 1990s when we served as vice-president and president of the Virginia State Board of Education. We oversaw the development of rigorous knowledge-based academic standards in English, math, science, and history, and the creation of standardized tests to assess academic achievement in grades 3, 5, 8, and at the end of high school courses. Accountability was applied equally to students and schools. After a phase-in period of ten years, students were required to "earn" the state's diploma by passing six high school level tests, and schools were required to "earn" the state's accreditation by maintaining an acceptable student pass-rate on the tests.

In countless public hearings throughout the state, parents and business people supported these reforms while Virginia Education Association members opposed them.

One Virginia state senator, who was also a public school administrator, lamented on the Senate floor, "Never have I seen so much attention given to student learning." Imagine that!

The NEA and its affiliates have spent millions of dollars annually and devoted countless hours to elect candidates who support their educational philosophy. Their members have promoted radical environmental, energy, and disarmament policies for American society and self-indulgent self-esteem, anti-Western multiculturalism, and peer counseling for students.

The NEA's near-neurotic preoccupation with sex has produced mandatory sex education—twelve years of it in some states. I've often thought that since even the dullest child is capable of understanding the basics of sex in a thirty or forty-five minute conversation, proponents of twelve years of sex classes for children should be required to explain the rest of their agenda for what they cagily call "Family Life."

Perhaps inevitably, the union's current initiative is to develop new "Gay, Lesbian, Bisexual and Transgender Education" curricula for all public schools. When do we hit bottom?

How much better off children would be today if the NEA had chosen to channel its energies and power into true educational excellence—early reading skills for every child, along with a good grasp of math and science, and an objective historical literacy. There would have been no statistics showing that one in three children read at "below basic" levels. And we probably wouldn't be witnessing the explosion of home schooling and school choice initiatives.

■ The NEA has consistently opposed parental school choice in all forms.

The NEA fought—and lost—the battle against home schooling. Today it is the primary litigant in legal actions to stop various state school choice tuition tax credits and voucher initiatives, even those like Florida's, designed only to rescue children from habitually failing public schools.

The union claims that it is merely protecting public schools, yet it opposes even charter schools, which are nothing more than public schools of choice.

In reality, the NEA has one objective: to protect its 150-year-old power structure. It represents the interests of its members very effectively, but children and families are not its members.

As a result, parents are at the forefront of the most important idea in education today—parental school choice.

Why, then, should school choice matter to those who don't have children in public schools?

1. Because it is the only way this nation is likely to achieve true reform and a true education renaissance—

A number of conservatives have asked me why I spend so much time on public schools when my own children have other options. But it is not that simple: 90 percent of America's children are in public schools, and most of the other 10 percent

The Milwaukee public schools were among the worst in the nation before the Milwaukee tax-supported voucher program brought real reform ten years ago.

are in private schools that are only slightly better. Let me explain.

The Milwaukee public schools were among the worst in the nation before the Milwaukee tax-supported voucher program brought real reform ten years ago. Giving 65,000 children a choice had a dramatic effect on education. It meant that public, private, and faith-based schools had to compete for customers. As a result, *all schools*—public and private—improved. Competition through school choice benefited everyone—children, schools, and society. It is a sterling example of the kind of educational renaissance this nation needs.

The reality of private school education in America is that, with some outstanding exceptions, most seek to stay just one notch or two ahead of public schools. Too many private schools follow the lead of the public schools in low achievement expectations, unproven teaching methodologies and curricula, and social engineering, such as sex ed, counseling, and mandatory community service.

In my family we have been equally disconcerted by what has gone on at both the private and public schools our three sons have attended. One high-priced private school bragged about its religious-based mission in its literature, but in actuality refused to allow the teaching of the Ten Commandments—even as a matter of pure knowledge, not faith— because it might "offend someone."

Likewise, when one son was in a public school sixth grade class, we were astounded to learn that the Thanksgiving week assignment was to write an essay on what it felt like to be the turkey. Even on Thanksgiving they had to find a victim for the children to write about. (My son told me that the savvy sixth graders joked privately that if they were the turkey first thing they would do is get a lawyer.)

Also, recall that most private school teachers have been trained in the same public university schools of education that have trained public school teachers—the number of teachers trained at private schools of education is really quite small.

Well then, some say, what you need is to home school your children. I have tremendous respect for home schooling parents and think they are incredibly dedicated. But temperament and economics play a big role in home schooling. Much as we love our children, God didn't make us all schoolteachers. And the level of government taxation on families, in most cases, just doesn't allow one parent to stay home and home school.

Some may think that if public schools deteriorate further, private and home schooling will flourish and school choice will prevail. But waiting for public schools to self-destruct seems like an odd path to educational excellence.

2. Because the nation can't tolerate the high failure rates that the public school is producing—

Twenty-five years from now the current generation will be assimilated into the economic and cultural life of the nation. How long can a nation survive if one in three young adults is functionally illiterate? Even if you home school or privately educate your children, what kind of a society will your children have to live in?

By being silent over decades while the public school monopoly demanded and received more power over the lives of children and a greater share of our wages, we have been accomplices to the *death of freedom* and the *rise of government as surrogate parents.*

3. Because public school spending is out of control—

If higher spending produced higher student and school performance, achievement should have risen dramatically over the past three decades. Spending on U.S. public schools rose from $3,645 in 1970 to $6,434 in 1995 (in real 1997 dollars) yet the National Assessment of Educational Progress (NAEP) reading scores for seventeen-year-olds during the same period remained virtually unchanged. Math scores for the same age group were only slightly better.

The higher spending/higher achievement theory was put to its ultimate test in 1985 when a federal court ordered a complete overhaul of Kansas City's public schools. Missouri's fourteen-year $2 billion experiment bought fifteen new schools, fifty-six magnet schools, state-of-the-art vocational training centers, a world-class athletics department that offered fencing instruction by a former Olympic team coach, a 40 percent increase in teachers' salaries, and a student/teacher ratio of 12 or 13 to 1.

When local taxpayers resisted tax increases to pay for the overhaul, the court ordered property tax rates doubled and imposed a 1.5 percent surcharge on wages earned in the city. Missouri was forced to spend 45 percent of its education funds on the 9 percent in Kansas City.

Nine years later when the federal court ended the project, white enrollment had declined, test scores hadn't improved, and the drop-out rate had increased to 60 percent. State accreditation of the Kansas City public schools was revoked in May 2000 when the schools failed to meet any of the eleven state educational performance measures.

Money can't buy real education improvement; only competition can bring that about.

4. Because the present system has become an elitist system—

Though one liberal Democrat, a wealthy businessman with whom I worked while on the Virginia State Board of Education, and I agreed on little else, we found common ground in our desire to improve academic rigor in public schools. After his children had spent a few years in failing Richmond city schools, he had chosen to send them to elite private schools.

In due course, we had a very telling conversation on the issue of school choice. He said he gave the public schools ten more years before giving up on the government-run system and doing his best to privatize the entire thing. He added that he thought that many liberal businessmen agreed with him.

I suggested that waiting ten years would ill serve an entire generation of children and asked why not institute a tuition tax credit or voucher system now in order to give all children the options our children enjoyed.

"Oh, Michelle," he said, "you don't really expect all children to have the same educational opportunities that our children have."

This comment really gets to the crux of much of the resistance to school choice, and by liberals who should know better. It is the ultimate in elitism to believe that children of the more affluent and influential families should naturally have a better education than children of the masses.

5. Because school choice is ultimately about freedom—the right of each to life, liberty, and the pursuit of happiness in his own terms—

In a nation where we cherish so many freedoms, we have denied ourselves the freedom to educate our own children. The extraordinary effects of freedom are apparent in our government and economy—in every aspect of our lives. We must apply this same freedom to the education of our children.

Remember the little boy who stood before the U.S. Supreme Court in February holding the sign that read, *Who died and left the government my parents?*

In essence, we have. By being silent over decades while the public school monopoly demanded and received more power over the lives of children and a greater share of our wages, we have been accomplices to the *death of freedom* and the *rise of government as surrogate parents*.

Ultimately, the battle for school choice is a battle for freedom—perhaps the most important one of our time. ■

A DOWNSIDE OF THE SEXUAL REVOLUTION THAT ACCOMPANIED FEMINISM IS THE COARSENING OF MALE-FEMALE RELATIONSHIPS. AS A RESULT A SUBCULTURE OF MEN HAS FOUND IT EASY TO BE SELF-INDULGENT AND IRRESPONSIBLE.

—SUZANNE FIELDS

MEN (AND WOMEN) BEHAVING BADLY

BY SUZANNE FIELDS
WASHINGTON, D.C., MAY 7, 1999
EXCERPTS FROM A SPEECH AT THE CONSERVATIVE WOMEN'S NETWORK

WE OFTEN HEAR FROM RADICAL FEMINISTS about how the world has to change so that women can be more successful and happy, but we hear much less about these matters from conservative women. I think there are several reasons for this.

Conservative women have generally been raised on the traditions that have been handed down through the ages which seem as obvious as the old wives tales passed on from generation to generation. Until modern times, giving birth was dangerous for both mother and child. Raising children was treacherous territory. Survival was hard. Motherhood was a full-time occupation, difficult and demanding. For centuries women did what they had to do to be responsible for their children. And men sometimes took advantage of a woman's physical vulnerabilities.

But except for certain artists and writers along the way, motherhood was rarely scorned by women until the twentieth century.

SUZANNE FIELDS writes a general interest column twice weekly for *The Washington Times*, which is syndicated nationally by the (Chicago) Tribune Media Services. She writes on cultural and political issues and holds a Ph.D. in English literature. She is the author of *Like Father, Like Daughter: How Father Shapes the Woman His Daughter Becomes*. She has two daughters and a son and lives with her husband Ted in Washington, D.C.

Simone de Beauvoir was the great-grandmother of contemporary feminism. Her book, *Second Sex,* the classic manifesto of
the liberated woman, was published in France in 1949 and in
the United States five years later. She dismissed a pregnant
woman as little more than an incubator.

A decade later Betty Friedan published *The Feminine
Mystique,* in which she wrote that suburban mothers with college degrees suffered from a disease without a name. Its symptoms were frustration, boredom, and a lack of personal identity. Gloria Steinem famously followed with the aphorism that
became a mantra of modern feminists: "A woman needs a man
like a fish needs a bicycle." (Years later, in her own sixties, she
discovered that fish sometimes do ride bicycles, and took a
husband.)

While post-feminism ushered in a backlash to much of this
nonsense, radical feminists on elite college campuses, by now
tenured professors, continue to give motherhood a hard time.
In women's studies courses, especially, it has not been politically correct for a young woman to say she yearns to be a mother more than a doctor, lawyer or women's studies professor.

I came of age in a transitional time before women's studies
was even a gleam in the eye of a Ph.D. I'm the mother of three
grown children, still married to my high-school sweetheart,
and I have a Ph.D. in English literature. I've been a newspaper
columnist since 1984. My personal experience illustrates the
complexities of feminism and family that women face today.

My father was a traditional father, a full-time breadwinner, and my mother, who worked before marriage, enjoyed being a full-time mother after my brother was born. I was born five years later. My father liked the role of protector, and my mother took pride in being "mom," cooking hearty meals (lots of roast beef and mashed potatoes) and knitting beautiful sweaters and afghans. She was a block warden during World War II, scouring our neighborhood to make sure all lights were out during air-raid drills, and when we needed her less as we grew up, she did volunteer work for charities. My father didn't want my mother to work and my parents felt lucky she didn't have to.

When I was growing up, a husband and wife, father and mother, understood their mutual obligations and responsibilities within the family. The larger culture supported traditional roles. In what seems crucial to me, my mother and father maintained traditional roles and even with the mundane tasks of raising children never lost their sense of romance. I remember my mother and father walking down the street holding hands.

When I was grown my father told me with a catch in his throat, "You know I really don't think I could have made it without your mom. She was the source of my strength." He never talked about "bonding" or "sexual attraction" or "relationships," but it was clear to me that my mother and father remained close even as they grew older and often moved in different directions in the world inside and outside the home. What was important was the way they lovingly played out those differences for my brother and me, as at the family dinner table every night.

During the years that I was growing up, marriage—not divorce—had the edge. Divorce was stigmatized. That held its own set of problems, but it also meant parents tried harder to stay together "because of the children."

I have a number of friends who were divorced in the 1960s and 1970s and many of them tell me that if "everybody" hadn't been getting a divorce, they probably wouldn't have, either. They began to feel that they may have merely exchanged one kind of perceived "unhappiness" for another. (When I tried to play match-maker for one of my divorced friends, I sometimes concluded that the only man I could think of to suit her was her former husband.)

I followed both a traditional and untraditional path in marriage which gives me a rather unusual perspective among many women today. I wasn't driven toward a career at first, but I always knew I would work. I earned a Ph.D. with three young children in tow. That wasn't always easy for them or for me or my husband, but it was my choice.

In retrospect, my husband and I both did a lot of growing up in our marriage because we were both only twenty-one when we married. We did not have children right away, which gave us a few years together before the overwhelming responsibilities of parenthood. Today men and women are marrying later and couples are having children later. The trade-offs are obvious. I know very young grandmothers who are glad they had their children early. Those decisions are very personal ones. The biological clock is a stern reminder that some choices run out.

Today cultural changes determine different choices, for better and for worse. The cultural edge is with career over motherhood. That's why so many mothers celebrate a day called "Take your daughter to work." But that's a superficial idea, at best.

> When I tried to play match-maker for one of my divorced friends, I sometimes concluded that the only man I could think of to suit her was her former husband.

No child gets even a hint of what real work is like on one day, any more than someone could get an idea of what motherhood is like by spending only one day at home.

Feminism has ushered in some positive choices for women, but radical feminism has limited others as well. A downside of the sexual revolution that accompanied feminism is the coarsening of male-female relationships. As a result a subculture of men has found it easy to be self-indulgent and irresponsible. It's from this group of men that I derived my original title: "Men Behaving Badly." I'm talking about men who do not take their responsibility to women or children seriously. I added women in parentheses because it became clear to me that women contribute to the problems they confront in men.

Stand-up comic Susan Easton says that one of her friends belongs to a men's group called, "Single Heterosexual Men Who Harbor No Hostility Toward Women." Asks Susan: "What is there, one member?"

"Men behaving very badly" was a metaphor in the nineties (when this essay was written). It was a striking headline in the *New York Times* in the summer of 1997, calling attention to an article about one of the nastiest contemporary movies on the theme of courtship, *In the Company of Men*. It's about two angry men whose sole purpose is to date a vulnerable young deaf woman, court her, take advantage of her naiveté and trust, and then dump her. The operative word is "dump," a word that became trendy as more men treated more women badly. I had never heard the word when I was in high school or college, but I hear many women using it today: "So he dumped me."

In a later movie called *Your Friends and Neighbors*, by the same director, women act as badly as men. Their relationships are gross and the betrayals are prolific. The two movies framed the dark side of romance at the end of the millennium, words set to the sound of the dissonant music of a farcical funeral march: This is how the sexual revolution ends, not with a bang, but with a whine and a whimper. In this scenario many women became equal opportunity sexual aggressors.

These were not great movies, but philosophically and intellectually they provoked. The director said that he personally trusts "traditional values" and makes these movies because he wants men and women to realize what has happened by trashing those values.

Ronald Reagan was ridiculed when he described women as the civilizing influence on men. Cartoonists caricatured him wearing a leopard skin, carrying a club, with his wife Nancy pulling him by the hair. Ridicule or not, his insight was right on. Women were, and are, the civilizing influence. When women gave up that role men began behaving badly and the culture approved. It was not all the fault of their testosterone.

> **The biological clock is a stern reminder that some choices run out.**

The changing culture and feminism loosened the traditional demands on men even as it freed choices for women. Every revolution brings its own set of compromises and is bound by the iron law of unintended consequences. The feminist revolution and the sexual revolution were powerful revolutions, and changed the way we articulate our desires.

The contemporary feminist revolution in this country began in the middle of the twentieth century, a considerable time after we got the vote. Women joined consciousness-raising groups, single-sex gatherings with a single theme: bad-mouthing men. Women spoke ill of the absent and the absentees were their dates, their steady boyfriends, their husbands and former husbands.

"The sexual revolution," writes feminist-fatale Camille Paglia, "has removed all kinds of protections from young women that male gallantry once provided." Women who wanted the pleasures of sexuality without commitment got what they asked for.

Freud said "Anatomy is destiny." It was a gross oversimplification, but when women decided to ignore the core of truth in Freud's remark they threw the baby out with the bathwater, literally and figuratively. As a result women often lose, big. You could ask any woman who hears that loud ticking of a biological clock, who desperately fears that time is running out on her ability to bear children.

Focus for a moment on the long view from 1950, and the birth of *Playboy* magazine. The theme of the *Playboy* philosophy, laid out at such length by Hugh Hefner, was a simple one: let men be boys. It was a magazine dedicated to fun. Real men, according to *Playboy*, no longer require marriage to affirm their masculinity. They could play at being boys, enjoying the hedonistic lifestyle of the sports car and the stereo and the glamorous figures they found in the whiskey ads in *Playboy*. They could fantasize about an airbrushed nude with a staple in her belly button. Then they could set out to find a real live nude of their own.

Playboy loved women, hated wives. The magazine made fun of alimony. Hence Barbara Ehrenreich, in *The Hearts of Men*, argues that the men who came of age through *Playboy* precipitated the breakdown in family values before modern feminism even came along. *Playboy* made irresponsibility glamorous, appealing to men who wanted to run away from commitment. What's bizarre about this happenstance is that twenty years after the first publication of *Playboy*, radical feminists rallied with men in their quest for independence, to the point of telling women that it was demeaning to take alimony, that freedom was worth the price of no-fault divorce.

Between the extremes of *Playboy's* philosophy and radical feminism, women and
men stopped looking at courtship, marriage, motherhood, fatherhood, family life,
and child-raising with the traditional
assumptions. It took the backlash of
impoverished victims of this change, aging
single childless women and single-parent
families headed by women, to get us to think again.

**The changing culture
and feminism loosened
the traditional
demands on men even
as it freed choices for
women.**

Perhaps the saddest victims of men who behave badly are
the fatherless children, abandoned by men. Boys who grow up
without a father repeat the cycle because that's the only model
they know. A daughter who grows up without a father is
unable to develop trust in that first man in her life, a deep
emotional wound for her future expectations of men.

As the dissatisfactions percolated in male-female relationships in the seventies and eighties, it was still difficult to speak
openly or get respectful media attention paid to these hidden
costs of radical feminism. The radical feminist "attitude"
lingers on college campuses today, and indeed thrives in the
faculty lounges.

I visited many college campuses in the nineties to talk about
family and feminism and the ensuing conflicts. Young women
who were imbued with the sensibilities of "women's studies"
asked a great deal of hostile questions. They didn't like full-time
motherhood for anybody (unless mother was a man). For these
women a career must come first for every woman. If someone

disagreed with that position, she better keep her mouth shut or she would experience the worst kind of stigmatizing.

I often voiced criticism of the one-note women in women's studies courses, but it was hard for anyone to come to my support. After my speech, however, many women came up to me to say, often in a whisper, "You know, I really agree with what you said, but I could never speak up. I wouldn't survive long on campus if I did." When that kind of attitude is pervasive, there is no dialogue, only emotional censorship. I speak and write often about romance, relationships, and courtship and I've discovered that many young women are totally unprepared to confront the contradictions in their lives. There's a craving for a mature dialogue on the subject.

As men saw that certain aspects of feminism played to their advantage, they joined forces in "equal opportunity." They decided that it was good for their finances, for their wives to work outside the home. Often both the man and the woman tested their "love" relationship by living together to see if they really wanted to get married. They chose to put off marriage for the sake of their careers. Someday, not today, maybe when little Tiffany and Brandon arrived, Mom could take a break, but only a short one, and then go back to work. The kids could be dropped off at a day-care center.

These attitudes were often mutually decided. But if—a big if—a woman changed her mind after having a baby and decided she didn't want to go back to work, well, that was not such a good idea. After all, they both depended on her paycheck as

much as his. Many women found themselves beyond the point of no return in their
relations with men, in their desire for full-
time motherhood.

I've had women confess to me that they
have become like the workaholic fathers
they railed against when they were growing up. They may want to enjoy the com-
panionship of men after work, even a little
pampering, but there's a slim chance for
that.

> After my speech, many
> women came up to me
> to say, often in a
> whisper, "You know, I
> really agree with what
> you said, but I could
> never speak up. I
> wouldn't survive long
> on campus if I did."

Typically, a professional woman will tell me she misses
being catered to by a man. She wants her mythical man to get
her tickets for the baseball game or the play, to ask her which
movie she wants to see, to tell her how pretty she is, to send
flowers and chocolates on days other than St. Valentine's Day.

These gestures have disappeared in certain quarters. The
first stage of romance is dissipated when sexuality takes over
too soon. "Cohabiting" is the big word in the modern
courtship vernacular. Cohabiting means living together without the blessing of judge or priest, preacher or rabbi. It also
means the "cohabitees" lack the blessings of their families and
friends who can lend crucial support to their choice of mate. A
number of women say the reason they cohabit is that they
don't want to divorce like their parents did. They think if they
get to know the guy better, by living with him as well as
sleeping with him before marriage, they'll have a greater

chance of marital success. Unfortunately, statistics prove otherwise. Those who cohabit before marriage have higher rates of
divorce than those who don't. Of course many of these couples
break up before marrying. It's easier to walk away when there's
no knot to untie.

I've found that many career women are pleased with their
professional lives, but find it difficult to turn off their aggressive work personalities and sink into a romantic mode with a
man in the evening. The softer side of femininity is harder to
get in touch with. Men react in kind. In the high-pressure
world in which many of us live, the cell phones, computers,
and answering machines are a convenience, but make it more
difficult to separate work and love.

Most women want what women have always wanted, marriage, motherhood, and grandmotherhood. They want to cherish and they want to be cherished. They want to nurture and
feel protected. They want to be independent and they want to
be cared for. But roles are so complex today that it is very hard
for a woman to unify the wishes held in the secret places of the
heart. Many women say that they do just fine living the life of
a singleton, but their voices have a slight bitterness.

As women and men are marrying later, the panic of not
marrying arrives later, too. That can be traumatic for a woman.
In the past three decades, according to the Census Bureau, the
proportion of twenty to twenty-four-year-old American
women who haven't married has doubled from 36 percent to
73 percent. Not so troubling, given that women are less

inclined to marry quite that young these days. But the number of unmarried women between thirty and thirty-four has more than tripled, from 6 percent to 22 percent. That's considerably more scary, particularly when biological clocks are ticking loudly and men refuse to hear them.

"When a woman postpones marriage and motherhood, she does not end up thinking about love less as she gets older, but more and more," writes Danielle Crittenden in *What Our Mothers Didn't Tell Us.*

Kate Worthie, in *Esquire* magazine (no less), writes the lament of the "retro-feminist" that reflects personally on the single life. "I live alone," she writes. "I pay my own bills. I fix my stereo when it breaks down, but sometimes it seems like my independence is in part an elaborately constructed façade that hides a more traditional feminine desire to be protected and to be provided for." The title of her piece was "The Independent Woman and Other Lies." She wanted men in *Esquire* to see beneath the veneer. But women must also look harder to see beneath the veneer, too.

"We often have to use feminine wiles to make love and work—work." Leslie Stahl, a reporter on CBS's *Sixty Minutes*, writes in her memoirs that working crushes female sexuality. It was an odd point coming from Ms. Stahl, since she used femininity to expand her professional role, getting a better interview, breaking down the defenses of a man resistant to her questions, but not to her charms.

Diane Sawyer, once America's Miss Junior Miss, does the

same thing. When she interviewed me in 1984, on my tour for my book, *Like Father, Like Daughter*, we talked about the importance of women being able to fuse competency and femininity. She looked at me with wide blue eyes and asked, "But isn't femininity what women have to leave behind?"

That may have been the public feminist position at the time, but I gave a resounding "No" even then. No one uses her femininity better than Diane Sawyer. ■

■   ■   ■   ■

POSTSCRIPT

Fast forward to 2002 to Paula Zahn, the CNN news personality who was outraged when a promotional commercial described her as "sexy." Anyone who can't see that she's sexy, with long shapely legs revealed by high hemlines and artful camera work, is blind or a hypocrite. Her seductive looks may not reduce the seriousness of her questions, but they often disarm the viewer and the person she interviews. The point here is that a lot of women mix femininity and competency to their professional advantage and there's nothing wrong with that except denying it.

Women must accept their responsibility for letting men behave badly. "Bridget Jones's Diary," the best-selling novel and a hit movie in 2001, tells the story of a thirty-something single woman in London who sums up her New Year's resolutions with a list of the men she must learn not to go out with: "alcoholics, workaholics, commitment phobics, people with girlfriends or wives, misogynists, megalomaniacs, chauvinists, freeloaders, perverts." She's trying to be funny, but the list cuts close to the bone of reality for a lot of single women her age. If a woman can't keep men from behaving badly, she has to try harder to keep one out of her life. And that's very, very sad.

There is a power-ful social stigma, thanks to the resounding success of the radical feminist movement, to being a stay-at-home mother.

—Kate Obenshain Griffin

GIVING IT UP *One Woman's Decision to Stay Home and Raise Her Children*

BY KATE OBENSHAIN GRIFFIN
WASHINGTON, D.C., JANUARY 7, 2000
EXCERPTS FROM A SPEECH AT THE CONSERVATIVE WOMEN'S NETWORK

I BELIEVE WITH ALL OF MY BEING that we as a society are making a tremendous mistake by allowing nannies and day-care workers to play such a fundamental role in raising our children. And I believe that my decision to stay home and raise my children was right, not just for me, but for many women whom our culture, thanks primarily to the radical feminist movement, has convinced otherwise.

Often I'm asked by those who know that I'm at home raising two little boys, "Do you work at all?"

I used to feel sheepish at their evident scorn, or at least bewildered. But now I say self-confidently, "No, I'm at home raising babies, full-time." When I assure them of my delight, the response is curt and invariably the same. "Oh, well, it's nice that you have that luxury." At this, I want to wave our tax returns from the past couple of years in their faces.

But let me tell you a little about myself, and how I came to my decision.

KATE GRIFFIN is a stay-at-home mother, freelance writer, and speaker. Prior to having her children she worked in Virginia Governor George Allen's administration, as lecture director for Young America's Foundation, served as vice chairman of the State Council of Higher Education for Virginia, and was a public policy consultant. She lives in Virginia with her husband, Phil, and three children.

When I was nine, my world came crashing down when my father was killed in an airplane accident while campaigning for the United States Senate from Virginia. From then on, my mother had to work to support her family. I wasn't brought up to be a stay-at-home mother. We children were thrown into what was an exhilarating and often addictive world of politics. And we learned early on how to be self-confident and knowledgeable on the issues. I was not trained in the fine arts of housekeeping and raising children, although my parents were deeply conservative and traditional.

Cutting my teeth in politics prepared me for a career in that arena. After college, I served as lecture director for Young America's Foundation and gained invaluable experience in public speaking. I also met some of the greatest and most influential conservative leaders of our time, including Bill Buckley and the late Russell Kirk. And I built what is now the largest conservative speaker's program in the country. But politics was in my blood, and all I needed was somebody to believe in, and I would get back into that world.

George Allen came along with fire in his belly and, I believed, the conservative principles that reminded me of my father. So I went to work for him. He won in a landslide, and I followed him to the governor's office, where I advised him on health and education issues.

Then, love came my way, and I married and moved to Winchester, Virginia, where my husband was a young lawyer. I began consulting on my own for campaigns, freelancing, and traveled occasionally to college campuses speaking on issues such as political correctness and feminism. And then, without much delay, Phil and I began a family.

It wasn't long before the consulting tapered off, and by the time our second son was born, I decided to commit myself completely to raising the children.

I do continue to serve in a volunteer capacity as vice chairman of the State Council of Higher Education for Virginia and I travel about one day a month, thanks to my gracious husband who takes time off to look after our children.

I do not want to overstate my career. In that regard, perhaps it was easier for me to make the decision to stay home than for women who are more established and wait before having children. I had a lot less to lose.

But psychiatrist John Bowlby got the point when he said that "young women with promising careers," like many of you in this room, "take a tremendous amount of pressure regarding what for them is the very difficult decision of whether or not to stay home and raise their children."

In any case, I decided to give up a career just as it was beginning to get exciting. I had earned a reputation in both the policy and political arenas and was in the perfect position to cash in.

Was I pressured by my husband to get out? No. He was none too pleased at the prospect of cutting our income by more than half. But as I came closer to motherhood, and then when my first child was born, I became convinced that the best I could do for the well-being of my family was to stay home to raise our children. I had been writing about the importance of family life since my college days, and as much as I enjoyed what I was doing, I believed it was time not just to talk the talk, but walk the walk.

Has it been easy? No, not always. There is a powerful social stigma, thanks to the resounding success of the radical feminist movement, to being a stay-at-home mother. Psychologist Michael Lamb said, "Especially in professional and middle-class circles, it is often rather shameful to admit to being only a housewife and mother."

I have felt the sting at cocktail parties when professionals, having discovered my primary occupation, made a quick exit from my company.

Do I feel fulfilled and stimulated as a stay at home mom? Do I feel appreciated? These needs have been touted by the feminist movement as only achievable in the workplace, and we as a culture have really bought into that. I've encountered many who say, "Oh, I wouldn't be happy or fulfilled staying at home, and that would not be good for the children. It's better that I work." If they were to ask their children about that, I wonder what they would say. It's as though society almost cannot stand the thought that some choose to raise their own children.

I experienced pressure to reenter the workforce in a very real way. I was about six months into my home career and still a bit uncertain when I received a call from a prominent member of the conservative movement. I was surprised and flattered. He informed me that a congressional commission was being formed, and he thought I should apply for the position of executive director.

I knew that this was a tremendous opportunity, and that with this on my resumé I could really go places.

Almost immediately, I forgot about the kids. I was swept up in the excitement of power and politics. Everyone—and I do mean everyone, even my mother who is a passionate believer in mothers staying at home—urged me to apply for the position.

> **It's as though society almost cannot stand the thought that some choose to raise their own children.**

There were two exceptions. One was Henry, my little boy, just on the verge of walking—clearly an opponent of the idea. And to my surprise, the other was my husband. Fatherhood had brought him a long way from the days when income was his primary concern. In the final analysis, he said, he could not imagine leaving Henry with anyone else. Additionally, he thought I would always regret the things that I missed while I was not at home. And he was absolutely right. I didn't apply for the position.

Now, I can honestly say that I don't believe I have given anything up. At a recent cocktail party someone said that I must have a real need to be considered important and useful.

But I do. It's hard to believe when you're in the workplace, particularly when your self-esteem is soaring, that you could ever be adequately fulfilled staying at home with small children.

No, you don't get the same rush. Rather, there is peace; peace in knowing that you are where you should be; peace in passing an afternoon quietly reading a story to a little one; peace in taking a leisurely afternoon stroll.

I titled this speech "Giving It All Up," but I don't believe I gave anything up. I believe I reaped far more from my decision to stay home than I ever would have had I stayed in my career.

I could be engaging in more intellectually stimulating exercises—policy research and development, writing papers and speeches—it's captivating, invigorating, and a little bit addictive. Instead, I wake up every morning about 5:30. I tiptoe downstairs, and I head out on a forty-five minute walk. I come home, jump in the shower, and try to squeeze in a quick cup of coffee with my husband, and chat about today's news. That's on a good day.

Usually, right before or right after the shower, I hear the pitter-patter of little feet, followed by, "Mommy, I'm ready to get up." Then our day is in full swing. But our day—that of Henry, Paul, and me—is becoming increasingly unique in our culture. There's no bundling up rushing off to day-care. I'm not scurrying around trying to find clean clothes to wear to work. Instead, we have our leisurely oatmeal and juice, and I face a day of diapers, naps, books, hugs, boo-boos, tears, and giggles.

I belt out all of my favorite tunes throughout the house. I read fairytales, play "ring around the roses," kiss bumps, tickle, and change an extraordinary number of diapers.

And there are scenes in my life, each of them like an epiphany or a reminder of why I do what I do, scenes when time seems to stand still. At those moments, my home is the center of the world, and I'm oblivious to anyone existing outside my sphere. At those times, my contentment is absolutely complete.

> I believe I reaped far more from my decsion to stay home than I ever would have had I stayed in my career.

My two-year-old could be playing happily on the floor with his trucks, occasionally looking up at me smiling, maybe sharing one of those stream of consciousness thoughts. I'll be sitting closely on the couch with my youngest sprawled on my lap, his warmth flowing freely. The last afternoon rays are streaming through my front door, and I have quiet music playing in the background. Something tells me that this is as it should be.

I'm not out there producing cutting-edge white papers. But God willing, I will help to mold these little ones in something we see less and less these days—responsible, generous, courteous, God-fearing, and productive citizens of this land that was built by men of those same traits.

Do I feel as if exciting things and changes are happening that I have no say in? No way. I have a stake in the future here. And I believe that I'm influencing it profoundly.

And when my children are older, I'll become involved again and try to influence our world in other ways. I do believe you can have it all, just not at the same time. And I also believe that after experiencing full-time what I see as the world's most fulfilling endeavor, motherhood, you may no longer want it all.

But thanks to the battlecry of radical feminism, quite a few women are determined to have it all, and right now. Fifty-nine percent of mothers with children under one and 65 percent with children under six are in the workforce, although not necessarily full-time.

Children are coming home to empty houses, either because they're a product of broken homes and their mothers must work, or because their parents must work to keep themselves above the poverty line, or all too often because their parents have certain economic standards and expectations. Or sometimes it is just because the mothers want to work, searching for true fulfillment anywhere but home.

But do we really find fulfillment in the workplace when someone else is looking after our children? Writer Kay Ebeling wrote, "The reality of feminism is a lot of frenzied and overworked women dropping kids off at daycare centers so they can rush off to jobs they don't even like." So is this just a personal decision or does it have broader social ramifications?

The nurturing, or lack thereof, that a child receives in the early years as he or she grows into the confusing times of preadolescence and adolescence will affect self-esteem, confidence, and the ability to learn and succeed. John Bowlby, the only psychiatrist to have received the American Psychiatric Association Highest Award twice, said that the attachment between baby and mother is "the foundation stone of personality. The young child's hunger for his mother's love and presence is as great as his hunger for food. And that if absent, inevitably generates a powerful sense of loss and anger."

To me it is just common sense that our children's sense of security will be largely determined by the response they receive from their parents. Are the parents, particularly the mothers, nurturing, encouraging, and responsive? Or are they worn out, preoccupied, and often absent?

> God willing, I will help to mold these little ones in something we see less and less these days—responsible, generous, courteous, God-fearing, and productive citizens.

What is the price we pay for children being left alone with no one to turn to for support and guidance except their peers, video games, or television, with all its incumbent messages of sex, drugs, alcohol, and violence? Hence the rise among teens in violence and death, drug and alcohol abuse, pregnancies and suicide, and the list goes on and on.

How tough is it to figure out that our kids need their parents? And they need them to be strong and unified, and, most importantly, present.

Recently the *Richmond Times Dispatch* ran an article about more professional moms opting to come home and raise their children. Karen Jackson was going to become the first female black astronaut, but she quit. Why? "My oldest son was having trouble in school. He was severely withdrawn and depressed. He had failed sixth grade. My son was fast becoming a statistic. He was another black male headed for trouble." After only nine months of home-schooling by his mother, her son went from testing at the fourth grade level to the ninth grade.

No one could say it better than former Milwaukee County Circuit Court judge, Leah Lamcone, who retired to stay home with her three sons. She said: "My decision to leave the bench after fourteen years was not easily made. Looking back on my years of both judge and mother, I have come to realize that the greatest impact I have made in any life is that which I've made in the lives of my children. While I suppose I could continue as both judge and mother, at age forty-four after the stress of a hard day, I doubt that I could be all the mother that two young boys and an infant deserve.

"I leave with alarm at what I have seen daily. I leave with a warning that we as a culture must end this cycle of procreation without committing to parenting dysfunctional household units and abdication to the government of the family's role in teaching moral, spiritual and social values."

And she concludes, "Hopefully, by investing more of my time in my own home, I will look up at the end of my life to see three young men emotionally vibrant and self-reliant, ready to face their life's drama. With that solid foundation, perhaps they will be better equipped to meet the challenge in their future of putting back together the pieces of society we let crumble in our hands." ■

In a good many Moslem and Hindu areas, even now, women not only have difficult lives, they have virtually unbearable lives.

—Dr. Jeane Kirkpatrick

Women Should Refuse to Choose Between Family and Career

BY DR. JEANE KIRKPATRICK
WASHINGTON, D.C., SEPTEMBER 15, 2000
EXCERPTS FROM A SPEECH AT THE CONSERVATIVE WOMEN'S NETWORK

BACK BEFORE THE THOUGHT was enveloped in political correctness—before that noxious notion had even been coined—I was interested in women's roles in society. Over a period of about five years, I spent almost all my time, professionally speaking, doing research and writing on women. I produced a couple of books, one called *Political Woman*, which was the first serious study in the modern period of women who entered the political arena, and stayed in it long enough to become influential in their legislatures.

In the same five-year period, I became deeply involved in studying the political behavior of both women and men, because whoever studied men would be studying women; otherwise, you wouldn't know whether anything you're studying

is relevant specifically to women. That study, *The New Presidential Elite*, was about the women and men who were

DR. JEANE KIRKPATRICK is a senior fellow at the American Enterprise Institute, and a Leavey Professor of Government at Georgetown University. The first woman appointed to serve as a Permanent Representative of the U.S. to the United Nations, she has written extensively on foreign policy and security affairs. The mother of three grown sons, she lives in Bethesda, Md.

delegates to the 1972 Democratic and Republican conventions. It was fascinating because 1972 was a fascinating year in American politics. It was the year that George McGovern ran and split the Democratic Party. I was myself a Democrat in those years, and part of a movement in the Democratic Party called the ABM movement, which meant Anybody But McGovern.

That year, 1972, split the Democratic Party to a degree that it never recovered. The full consequences of it were not clear until Ronald Reagan provided a viable, attractive alternative for everybody, including a good many Democrats, in 1980. The Democratic Party was especially interesting to women that year because the Democrats had adopted a quota system—the rule that there must be as many women delegates to the Democratic Convention as there were male Republican delegates to their convention.

You have to forgive my archaic use of such terms as women and men, male and female. I only learned yesterday, from one of the representatives of the Holy See to some current UN conferences, that it has been recently decided that there are at least five genders. Designation of any of those genders by such terms as male and female, woman and man, is passé, uninformed, and insulting to everyone, of whatever gender.

The world has changed a great deal since 1972. It's changed more rapidly and more dramatically than any of us fully realize. I have a favorite feminist classic, an essay by Virginia Woolf. In it Virginia Woolf undertook to explain to herself, as well as her readers, why women had achieved so little in certain fields. Why, for example, there had never been a great female writer or a great female composer or a great female scientist in centuries past.

She began by noting that it would have been completely and entirely impossible for any woman to have written the plays of Shakespeare, in the age of Shakespeare. And she explained why. Suppose, she said, Shakespeare had had a wonderfully gifted sister, Judith. What would have happened to Judith Shakespeare?

Well, Virginia Woolf said, Brother William was sent to school, where he learned Latin, grammar, logic, and read the masters in world literature. He lived adventurously, shot rabbits and deer, fathered a child while he was still quite young, and soon thereafter set off to the city to seek his fortune. He promptly procured a low-level job in a London theater, and set about learning the terms of his craft.

But Judith? Her life unfolded very differently. Judith was not sent to school, and had no chance of learning grammar, or logic, or coming to know great literature. When from time to time she picked up a book, she was probably interrupted by a request that she mend socks or do some other household chore.

When Judith was only sixteen, her parents contracted a marriage for her, and she resisted. For this, she was beaten and shamed. Nonetheless, in an act of extreme disobedience, Judith Shakespeare ran away to London. She, too, wanted freedom, but her efforts met with only scorn, until finally, she met a sympathetic stage manager, who befriended her. He was also attractive, and by him she soon became pregnant.

Not long thereafter, finding herself abandoned, disgraced, penniless, and jobless, Judith Shakespeare took her own life, leaving no trace of her extraordinary talent.

Of this scenario, Virginia Woolf wrote: "Any woman born with a great gift in the 16th century would certainly have gone crazy, shot herself, or ended her days in some lonely cottage outside the village, half witch, half wizard, feared and mocked."

Of course, Virginia Woolf intended Shakespeare's sister to stand for a long line of heroines who, abused and abandoned, strayed too far off the narrow pathway of one prescribed world onto the next. Undereducated, credulous young women in search of autonomy, they ended sooner rather than later, seduced, pregnant, abandoned, dead by their own hand.

That sounds dramatic, but it is also the truth. And the truth that's important is the narrow, narrow, narrow constraints in which almost all women, in almost all history, have lived their lives.

In today's world, in the Western world, at least, this seems incredibly far-fetched. But in a good many Moslem and Hindu areas, even now, women not only have difficult lives, they have virtually unbearable lives.

In 1975, during International Women's Year, the State Department asked me to lecture in West Africa. It was the year that my book *Political Women* appeared, and I spoke French. It was a searing experience for me. I didn't really real-

ize until that trip that Africa was overwhelmingly polygamous. Typically, their
men have four wives, and typically, girls
are virtually sold into marriage; they are
given or committed to marriage at very
young ages—eleven, even nine.

And they have literally no rights. In
many Moslem areas they had no right to
own property, no right to inherit a portion

> The truth that's important is the narrow, narrow, narrow constraints in which almost all women, in almost all history, have lived their lives.

of their husband's or the family's goods when the husband dies.
In a number of countries (men commonly have four wives) the
widow—rather, all the widows—inherit together one-fourth
of the total goods of the family. They basically live by begging,
or by attaching themselves to one or another of the brothers.
This is incredibly painful to watch.

I don't know whether you recall the refugee camps in the
Khyber Pass during the period when the mujahideen in
Afghanistan were fighting the Soviet invaders. About a million and a half, largely women, peopled those camps, because
most of the men had been killed, lost in the fighting, or captured. The women were without a man to protect them. We in
our "enlightened" Western culture had decided that we wanted to respect traditional cultures, and so we followed the traditional path of recognizing only males as legal persons.
Therefore, only males were registered to get ration cards.
Without which, you didn't get food. And only males were
educated in Koranic schools like those that trained the

Taliban, who went on to abuse women and girls in a systematic fashion. In those camps, and under our very eyes, they denied rights to females, all rights, including any kind of privacy. This was a harsh and terrible situation.

I've traveled and spent a lot of time in the Third World. I remember well that in Bombay, I saw a nine-year-old girl being sold into prostitution by her own family. This puts a rather dramatic perspective on rights, on basic rights, on women's rights, and on our concept of right and wrong.

All my life I have believed that it was appropriate and right that women and girls should be able to do anything that they were able, so to speak, and desired to do. Unfortunately, the capacity to perform a task or function doesn't necessarily accompany the desire. Having a right, for example, to compose music or write great literature doesn't necessarily give one the capacity.

But what can be especially tragic is when there is a capacity present without a right, when there are non-natural obstacles that prevent the development of God-given talents.

But back to the Western world. I think that American women, and Western women generally, are still living through a genuine revolution. If you look at the statistics on women's education in the United States, on the number of females in schools of medicine, law, engineering, and business, you see that revolution before your eyes.

And if you look at the number of American women who have entered the workforce over the last thirty-five or forty years, you see that revolution. This very dramatic change has, of course, brought with it an explosion of opportunity that in turn has led to an explosion of desires and ambitions, and some confusion. Because the existence of opportunity doesn't mean that it's going to be easily utilized. And the existence of ambition doesn't mean that it's going to be readily realized.

And only males were educated in Koranic schools like those that trained the Taliban, who went on to abuse women and girls in a systematic fashion.

I have been married for forty years to a political science professor. We had three sons, sadly, no daughter. Then after *Political Woman* was published, I did some speaking. At the time, colleges were beginning to come under some pressure to provide resources for girls in the athletic programs in schools. And people would ask me if I believed that women or girls should be able to play football along with the guys. I had a standard response to that. I began by saying I believed that women should be able to do anything they desired and were able to do. Then I would tell them about my football playing son, a weightlifter, strong and aggressive, characteristics essential to the game. If a girl wanted to come up against him on the football field, I told her I thought she would be out of her cotton-picking mind.

THE OTHER POINT I MADE WAS that I think that all of us, each and every one of us is bound by the constraints of nature. And these constraints of nature become confused in our minds with arbitrary social constraints, which are often obnoxious; I'm in favor of eliminating them. But sometimes, it's a little difficult to distinguish between what's arbitrary and what's not. Recently, *The Washington Times* carried a story about an officer in the Pentagon who is seeking to eliminate urinals. This is a good example of confusion about the difference between the constraints of nature and the constraints of the Pentagon. It is terribly important when you think about women's roles.

People have often said to me, what did I do that was the most interesting thing in my life. The answer is having a baby. That was by far the most important, exciting experience of my life. Having and raising babies is more interesting than making speeches at the United Nations. Believe me.

Sometimes you can't do everything, and if you can't make speeches at the UN, maybe you have babies, and if you can't have babies, maybe you make speeches at the UN. And if you're patient, and you prepare carefully you may be able to do both. More and more, we find women who are attempting both traditional and professional roles—not necessarily at the same time, but in the same lifetime. You can make it work. It takes a little luck and a lot of work. Both are very important.

American women today are breaking all kinds of boundaries and borders, and enriching our society in the process. I would like to see more women in influential roles in our society. And although I'm a partisan and an active Republican, I was delighted when Madeleine Albright rose to the heights of leadership as secretary of state. And I'm gratified that Donna

Shalala has done a respectable professional job as secretary of health and human services.

Both of them are political scientists, attaining their Ph.D.s at a time when not many women were even attempting such distinctions. There's a certain truth in Jesse Jackson's assertion that when one barrier is broken, other barriers get broken.

I like to tell this story about my own personal experiences at the White House. After I was appointed to be the U.S. representative to the United Nations, I came to realize that, not only was I the first American woman to be the U.S. permanent representative to the UN, but that no woman in the Western world had ever been her country's principal representative to the UN. There have been women ambassadors and representatives, but no principals, which is what we call permanent representatives of a country for the United Nations. My appointment was a big shock to most of the members of the UN because most of them came from societies that had little respect for the very concept of women's rights.

Then it dawned on me that I was the first woman who had ever been appointed to a post that put me, as they say in government, at the table where the top decisions in foreign policy and national security are made. There had never been a woman secretary of defense, or state, or filling any of the senior positions.

This still was sinking in one day when I was in a meeting of the National Security Planning Group, the NSPG. It was the most inner group of decision-makers in the Reagan administration and consisted of the president, vice president, secretary of state, secretary of defense, national security advisor, head of the CIA, and military chief of staff. This is where the big debates took place, where the biggest decisions were made. The president presided. Often he made decisions on the spot.

There were about eight people around the table, which was in the basement of the White House. The super-secure room had heavy doors and special Marine guards who sat outside with their guns at the ready. They kept the door locked and had to formally recognize you before they unlocked the door to let you in.

So there we were, sitting in this room, discussing an issue of high importance to the United States when suddenly Cap Weinberger, the secretary of defense, said, "It's a mouse!" "In the Situation Room?" said Bill Casey. "A mouse in the Situation Room?" Somebody else said, "Is it a real mouse?" And then another voice, "How did a mouse get into the Situation Room?" Well, we looked at the mouse, the mouse looked at us, and the mouse walked across the room and disappeared.

Insofar as I know, nobody ever knew how the mouse got in, or how the mouse got out.

Like that mouse, you can't tell where you may end up, if you do your lessons and you work hard. ■

THERE ARE TWO WAYS THAT AN OPPRESSOR OR A DICTATOR CAN CONTROL THE PEOPLE— THROUGH PHYSICAL OPPRES- SION AND THROUGH CONTROL- LING PRIVATE PROPERTY.

—NANCIE MARZULLA

PROPERTY RIGHTS VS. GOVERNMENT REGULATION:

More at Stake Than Just Your Backyard

BY NANCIE MARZULLA
WASHINGTON, D.C., NOVEMBER 19, 1999
EXCERPTS FROM A SPEECH AT THE CONSERVATIVE WOMEN'S NETWORK

ANY DISCUSSION ABOUT PROPERTY RIGHTS should start by going back to the Constitution. James Madison, who drafted our Bill of Rights, at the insistence of the states, demanded that there be some protections for individual rights and states' rights. Thus, in the Bill of Rights you find protections for private property rights in both the Fourth and the Fifth Amendments. Thomas Jefferson identified property rights in the Declaration of Independence when he asserted that the proper role of government is to protect its citizens' life, liberty, and pursuit of happiness. Jefferson's writings make clear that by "pursuit of happiness" he didn't mean something like the 1970's notion of "anything goes," or "if it feels good, do it," or the 1990's fixation with instant gratification. Rather, he

meant something more along the lines of the right to enjoy the fruits of one's

NANCIE G. MARZULLA is a founder and president of Defenders of Property Rights. She was an appointee in the Reagan Justice Department. She practices regularly before the Supreme Court and federal courts, and has testified before the U.S. House of Representatives and the U.S. Senate. She is co-author of *Property Rights: Understanding Government Takings and Environmental Regulation.* She lives in Washington, D.C., with her husband, Roger, and two children.

labor, or what we think of today and describe simply as private property rights. In fact, Jefferson's original draft borrowed John Locke's formulation: life, liberty, and property.

Why did our Founding Fathers place so much emphasis on protecting private property rights? Because they understood that there are essentially two ways that an oppressor or a dictator can control the people. The first is through physical oppression. The other is through controlling private property. We can see very easily how liberty is destroyed by looking no farther than the former Soviet Union, whose government controlled the citizens and allocated everything—apartments, cars, careers, educational opportunities—everything.

Our Constitution, on the other hand, by guaranteeing the right to own and use private property, secures for us our homes, our jobs, our educational opportunities, and our right to enjoy the fruit of our labor. In short, our property rights are secured against government destruction.

The current controversy over this important constitutional right arose directly out of the Fifth Amendment's requirement contained in the just compensation clause, which states, "nor shall private property be taken for public use without payment of just compensation." That's the crux of what this modern controversy over property rights centers around.

And this is because, in its most simple terms, the government wants more property, more land, more power, than it can pay for. Its appetite for more—more land, more forms, different kinds of property—is unlimited. The only thing standing in the government's way is this "loathsome" requirement that it has to pay for what it takes.

I would like to focus our discussion of property rights on the woman's perspective, which may really be what counts the most; because what women believe about property rights may be pivotal concerning this key constitutional right in the coming years. I'll explain in a moment.

Let me say now that despite the fact that the Constitution placed enormous emphasis on protecting private property rights, there is not a single law on the books implementing this constitutional right. Think about the other rights mentioned in the Bill of Rights; many of these provisions have elaborate implementation programs in various statutes and regulatory programs. Take the Equal Protection Clause: you need think no further than Title VII, Title VIII, fair employment, fair housing programs, the Voting Right Acts, and so forth, to realize to what lengths Congress has gone to implement those protections over due process, criminal rights, excessive fines, and the rest. In many instances, Congress has stepped in and demanded that government exercise its powers in such a way as to conform with what the Constitution requires.

But with respect to the just compensation clause, Congress has done nothing. On the contrary, we have a veritable explosion of laws that adversely affect private property rights. For example, the Clean Air Act, the Surface Mining Control and Reclamation Act, the Coastal Zone Management Act, the

Super Fund, FIFRA, the Endangered Species Act, the Federal Wetlands Regulatory Program—all of these federal laws and regulatory regimes have had enormous negative impacts on private property rights. There are hundreds of thousands of pages of rules and regulations of all sorts, of all varieties, on all topics, that adversely affect private property rights. But not a single page is devoted to protecting private property rights.

In fact, no activity, no human endeavor is more heavily regulated than the use of private property in our society. Added to the federal level, there are the various state regulatory regimes, not to mention local government land use and zoning controls. In short, the unconstitutional taking of private property is an epidemic in this country.

This wholesale destruction of our liberty can only be stopped if we can come up with leaders who are willing to stand up for the property rights of the people. Agency bureaucrats can be made to obey the Constitution only if Congress requires them to do so; for example, by conducting meaningful oversight hearings, changing environmental laws, and enacting strong property rights legislation. There have in fact been a number of really excellent property rights proposals introduced in Congress since 1990. What is missing is not the proposals, but the political will to enact them.

We all know that political leaders may not read the Constitution, but they always read the polls. And what the polls tell us today is that the female voter—I'm finally back to women!—between the ages of twenty-one and fifty are the most influential and sought-after segment of the voting population. Indeed, how you vote in the coming years will determine every election from the presidency on down. Therefore, what you have to say about this issue will really count. That is,

We have a veritable explosion of laws that adversely affect private property rights.

the political leaders you elect, and their stance on property rights, will be critical in deciding whether the government will conduct its business the constitutional way or continue down the path from freedom to socialism.

The home and the family are top priorities for women, as are educational and career opportunities. In other words, what women want reads like something out of the Federalist Papers. They want the pursuit of happiness as understood by Thomas Jefferson, James Madison, and our Founding Fathers. And the only way women are going to be able to achieve these goals is, again, through the protection of private property rights.

It may be dead white men who wrote the Constitution, but the fight to protect our liberties is being led, believe it or not, by women. For example, Jean Nollan.

The Nollan decision that was rendered by the Supreme Court in 1987 forms part of what we refer to as the 1987 Trilogy. Another dauntless woman, Florence Dolan, took the city of Togard, Oregon, all the way to the Supreme Court because it had grabbed a swathe of her beachfront property, declaring it a public easement, a public pathway, without payment of just compensation. The U.S. Supreme Court struck the taking down as invalid, using the just compensation clause as a sword, which is an astonishing way to view the just compensation clause, because many people see it simply as a money-mandating provision.

Another important case was recently won by Bernadine Suitam. She battled the Tahoe Regional Planning Authority for permission to use her property. In her case, the government opposed even her right to go to court. When she finally got to the Supreme Court, she had to be carried in a wheelchair—she was in a wheelchair and blind by then. But she won her case. She got her day in court, and eventually obtained just compensation for the taking of her property.

In another case, Mary and John McMachin built a vacation home on dry land. The Corps of Engineers, however, said it was wet—but not until after the McMachins had built the house and lived in it for three years. The government wanted them to tear down the house, or move the house—but the McMachins refused. Through litigation, the government was forced to give them an after-the-fact permit.

Jeannie Ebram is another gutsy person, a grandmother with five grandchildren. This picture of the back of her vacation home is important because next to the little cement area you'll see green grass. Today the grass is gone because there was a storm on the coastline of Texas that tore up the grass. Well, guess what Texas law now says? Because there's no vegetation next to the house, the land has become beach land, publicly owned land, and she has to move her house off of state property. In fact, she's going to be fined for having personal property on public property if she doesn't move her house immediately. But this woman is not willing to roll over and play dead. She wants to fight this case. And so we are suing the state of Texas.

It may be dead white men who wrote the Constitution, but the fight to protect our liberties is being led by women.

Hilda Taylor is another woman whom we are currently involved with. She has Parkinson's disease and needs a home that will accommodate her wheelchair. She currently lives in a two-story house. Her husband, a builder, would like to build her one on a lot they own in Fairfax County, Virginia, but the U.S. Fish and Wildlife service says no because the lot is located adjacent to a bald eagle's nest. The bald eagle has been taken off the Endangered Species Act list, or is supposed to be taken off, as proclaimed by President Clinton, because the bird is no longer in danger. But the Fish and Wildlife Service is telling the court that Mr. Taylor can't build his house because technically the bird is still on the list.

I could go on the rest of the afternoon talking about these women litigants, but I'll end with Kathy Stupak Thrall. This woman is a real property rights warrior. She was a property owner who had a home by a lake in Michigan. Everything was fine. I don't think she ever thought about private property rights. But then the federal government came along and told them that they couldn't use the lake anymore because the lake was adjacent to federal land. And according to the federal government it can control adjacent property because there has to be a buffer around federal land, and if it destroys private rights that exist in the use of the lake, it's just too bad. It's something that the federal government thinks it's entitled to. But Kathy Stupak Thrall thought otherwise, and took the federal government to court. Unfortunately, the Circuit Court of Appeals that heard the case did not agree, but that did not stop Kathy; in fact, I think it just got her started. Because now she's running for public office and trying to get the laws changed to put an end to such thefts of private property. I predict that we're going to be hearing more from Kathy Stupak Thrall.

Let me close by touching on a topic that I have been asked to discuss, which is about success and conservative women in the fields of litigation. To my mind, thinking about success is not a very good way of going about one's life. More helpful and more useful to me is what Mother Teresa said, which is, "We are not called upon to be successful. We are called upon to be faithful." That is what I would recommend to anyone who was making life choices.

What in life brings the most satisfaction and the most meaning is making decisions and living your life faithful to your duties and responsibilities as a wife, a mother, a friend, a professional, and being faithful to your God. Live your life in such a way and your life will count for something that's bigger than yourself.

Making decisions in order to build your resume or get an

award does not bring much personal happiness or satisfaction, and it certainly doesn't make the world a better place to live in. The women I've just mentioned left the comforts of everyday life and took on the really arduous task of suing the government to protect our rights, for something bigger than themselves. ■

THE PLAN IS FOR POLITICIANS IN 2013 TO DIP INTO THE TRUST FUND IN ORDER TO PAY BENEFITS. THAT, HOWEVER, IS WHEN SOME PEOPLE SAY THE CRISIS STARTS. BECAUSE THE MONEY WON'T BE THERE.

—DARCY OLSEN

WOMEN AND SOCIAL SECURITY: *Real Strategies to Change the Future*

BY DARCY OLSEN
WASHINGTON, D.C., MARCH 12, 1999
EXCERPTS FROM A SPEECH AT THE CONSERVATIVE WOMEN'S NETWORK

THERE'S A SCENE IN A MONTY PYTHON episode where a king and his son are standing in front of a huge castle. The father wants to leave the castle to his son and relates this to his son: "Son, they told me I couldn't build a castle in a swamp, but I did, and it sank into the swamp. So then I built a second castle, and it, too, sank into the swamp. But, undeterred, I built a third castle, and it burned down...and sank into the swamp. But this, this is the fourth castle, and this one is the best in the land, and this is the one I am giving to you." But the son just looks at him, dolefully; he obviously wants nothing to do with the castle. Because what good is something that's fated to fall into the swamp?

This is a good picture of Social Security today. Social Security is unsustainable because it has a structurally unsound foundation, very

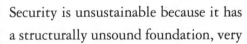

DARCY OLSEN is executive director of the Goldwater Institute. She guides the research, supervises scholars and staff, is chief spokesperson, directs fundraising, and manages business affairs. Previously Olsen served as director of Education and Child Policy at the Washington, D.C.-based Cato Institute. She holds a BA from the School of Foreign Service at Georgetown University and a master's in international education from New York University.

much like the swamp, any swamp. It is called a pay-as-you-go system. Which is why Social Security is necessarily flawed, why it is falling apart. The question is, how can you build it with a firm foundation that will last?

Right now, all workers pay a 12.4 percent payroll tax—whether rich or poor, and no matter what you earn; it's a tax on the very first dollar you earn. But when you pay that money to Social Security, it doesn't go into any kind of insurance or retirement account for you. Instead it goes immediately to pay the benefits of today's retirees. Nothing, that is, is being saved or invested for your future. We can only hope that when we get to retirement age there will be enough young workers to pay enough taxes for us to get our benefits. But the trouble with that is that there are fewer and fewer workers, and more and more retirees.

This is what is called the demographic problem. In 1950, for example, you had sixteen workers supporting each retiree—that is sixteen people paying taxes for each retiree. That worked fine. But today there are about three workers supporting each retiree, and in 2025 there will be about two to one. The demographic problem means we have many people to support and very few young workers to support them.

In comes the so-called surplus, which has supposedly been accumulating in what is called the trust fund. The plan is for politicians in 2013 to dip into that trust fund in order to pay benefits. That, however, is when some people say the crisis starts. Because the money won't be there. It will have been spent on other government programs and replaced with bonds. Unfortunately, bonds don't really count as real cash because there are only three ways to cash those bonds: (1) raise taxes, (2) cut benefits, (3) issue new debt. In short, the government can raise taxes or cut benefits. One indirect way of

> **As bad as the future looks for all workers, especially all young workers, it's even worse for women.**

handling this is by raising the retirement age, which is very unpopular for obvious reasons. Another direct way is to cut people's benefits. Which is even more unpopular, for even more obvious reasons.

As if that were not enough, there are real problems with Social Security apart from the financial crisis, and they affect young workers. The first woman to retire from Social Security, Ida Mae Fuller, paid $44 into the system and received thirty-five years of benefits. For her, it was a stellar investment. Young people today, however, can expect a negative rate of return. For example, an African-American male born after 1959 faces a negative real rate of return. Part of this is life expectancy, but only part. Basically, for every dollar he pays he gets about 88 cents back. This is the kind of investment that nobody in his or her right mind would ever choose if they had the freedom to do otherwise. Gen X has been left with a big problem.

Now, as bad as the future looks for all workers, especially young workers, it's even worse for women. And for a couple of reasons. The main reason is called the dual entitlement rule.

Simplified, it means that you can collect benefits in three different ways. The first is as a worker. If you work and never marry, you will get benefits. The second way is as a spouse. If you marry and never work—which happens but not often anymore—you can get 50 percent of your husband's benefits—whether or not you've ever paid into the system. The third way is as a worker and a spouse. As such, it seems as if you would be entitled to both. But you can't get both, you can only get the higher of the two benefits. And since husbands have higher salaries than many of their working wives, what the women have contributed counts for nothing, nothing at all. They are just as well off as if they had never entered the workforce, all their contributions are wasted.

That injustice happens to 25 percent of us. In about forty years, almost half of us will be affected in this way. By contrast, in personal retirement accounts, every dollar earned by a woman would work for her. And that's a big difference.

Although Social Security on its face is structured to be neutral it has built-in discriminations. Any way you look at it, women are worse off than men under Social Security. The average woman's benefit is only about $600 a month. For many women, that's all they have to live on. The average man's benefit is about $810. What you end up with is a poverty rate among women that is twice as high as it is among men. The poverty rates among women are about 13 percent, among black and Hispanic women about 29-30 percent.

And yet you hear that Social Security keeps people from

poverty. Well, it doesn't. I argue that in many ways it keeps people in poverty, because if you are a low-wage worker, and you earn $10,000 or $12,000 a year, and you pay 12.4 percent of your income in a payroll tax, you don't have a lot left over to save no matter how hard you pinch your pennies. Social Security takes this 12.4 percent, and gives you a negative rate of return, whereas if you were able to invest, even in bonds, you could get a 3 percent or a 4 percent return, or in the market perhaps 7 percent. Social Security contributes to the poverty rates because it prevents women from saving money they would otherwise have available to save—money they earned.

> And yet you hear that Social Security keeps people from poverty. Well, it doesn't. I argue that in many ways it keeps people in poverty.

The good news is that it could be different. In a recent study, we at Cato did two things. We looked retrospectively at women who retired in 1981 and compared what they could have gotten had they invested in the market with what they actually received from Social Security. We found that widows would have been two times better off given actual market returns; wives four times better off; and single women one-and-a-half times better off. Single women almost always have it the roughest because they don't have any earnings sharing.

Then we did a prospective analysis—these are the ones you more commonly see: What would it look like in the future if...? So assume you take 10 percent of the payroll tax, you invest it in accounts, they're earning a 6.2 percent rate of return—which is more than 1 percent lower than what the market has actually returned over the past seventy-five years; i.e., it leaves some room for serious error—for administrative costs, and so on. In this scenario the average woman would have an average of $833 more a month when she retires—more than *twice* what Social Security promises (but doesn't yet have the money to pay for). That is the difference between poverty and comfort in retirement.

We've designed a system that really could eliminate poverty because not only would we allow workers to take 10 percent of the 12.4 percent and put it into these personal retirement accounts, but if for some reason you didn't accumulate enough in your account to retire (the government would set that level), if, that is, you only had $80 and you needed $100, the government would top it off with funds from general revenue. In effect, nobody would ever have to fall below the poverty line. I don't think you'd really need the government safety net, because of what we've seen from the returns, but it could be built in, just in case.

The other good thing about this is that if you allow low-income workers to get a good, secure retirement from this money, they don't have to try to set aside what little they have; they can free up money for other things, like buying a home, or educating a child, or health care or whatever else.

Yet another reason is ownership. The ownership component is one of the most important. When you, liberal or conservative or somewhere in between, get to retirement, nobody wants to go to the government and put his or her hand out and say, "Will you hand me my retirement check?" People feel much better about themselves and more secure about their retirement if they've got the money in the bank and control their own incomes. It is time that people, rather than politicians, actually be in control of their retirement. The ownership element is absolutely critical.

Something else important about ownership is that, in the current system, if you die when you're sixty-four years old and you don't have any children under age eighteen nor a spouse that would get a survivor's benefit, all of your money is gone. If you had a private system, you could pass that money on to your church, to your nephews, to your friends.

Another reason personal accounts are right for workers is because it would be wrong to tell someone who depends on a $600-a-month check that you're going to cut it down to $400 because the young people can't afford to pay the higher rate. Our way, you can ensure retirement for the elderly while protecting the young from unfair tax burdens. Ethically, it rings true.

Finally, this plan will increase our freedom to make our own decisions about retirement. While this system would be mandatory initially, if, over time, the politicians would learn that we actually can save, we may gain complete freedom from this mandatory system in the future.

One thing is for sure: If the people had been given control over their retirement savings and their money from the very beginning, we wouldn't have our present $9 trillion debt or an unfunded liability. A plan the Clinton administration floated at one point to alleviate the situation was government investing. But, in short, government investing is socialism, not capitalism, and the American people intuitively don't like it. There are concrete reasons as well. For one, it does nothing to give people ownership, which is very important. For another, it gives the government a complete open door to walk in and start paying off its supporters by investing in their companies.

Another problem is that, in general, publicly invested funds have 2 percent lower returns than privately invested funds, because they are politically manipulated. If you look at pension funds across the states, 42 percent of them have socially correct or politically targeted investments. They cannot invest certain funds that involve, say, South Africa as it was, or Ireland, or Afghanistan, or Iraq, and so on. And then there are the rules about where you have to invest—in public housing projects, in monolithic community centers, in racial or ethnic or secular this and that. So you get lower returns. And if you think there's been a lot of this kind of corruption at the state level, imagine how bad it will be with 535 politicians in Washington who are completely removed from the elective process! Government investing is not a good idea.

I won't go into budget accounting—buying down the debt and so on—except to say that it does nothing to change the ominous 2013 date. Suffice it to say that President Clinton's own comptroller, and the head of the CBO, and Alan Greenspan—all of the leading authorities on budget and economic issues—have said that this plan doesn't put off the day of reckoning.

The bottom line in this debate—and it is a debate—is that it's your money and your future and it should be your choice. It is just that simple. ■

AS LATE AS 1965, 78 PERCENT OF BLACK HUSBANDS WERE IN THEIR HOMES WITH THEIR FAMILIES, DESPITE RACISM AND POVERTY. THEN CAME THE GREAT SOCIETY, AND THE ILLEGITIMACY RATES IN BLACK AMERICA SOARED TO 70 PERCENT.

—STAR PARKER

My Struggle from Welfare to Independence

BY STAR PARKER
WASHINGTON, D.C., APRIL 6, 2001
EXCERPTS FROM A SPEECH AT THE CONSERVATIVE WOMEN'S NETWORK

ENTHUSIASM. I CAN SEE IT IN YOUR FACES. It means a lot in my work. When I go to housing projects to deliver our message, I'm met with a lot of enthusiasm because the girls are looking to get out of the situation that we've sent them into; many of them read my book and say, "Gosh, if you can do it, I can do it." I did it because God took me out of a life of drug activity, criminal activity, and sexual abuse that led me into the abortion clinics over and over again. Finally, one day, I had a gut instinct way down deep that there was something wrong with killing your offspring. So I have a kid and the best thing around is welfare, and I end up in that system for years until one day I meet everyday folks, working in a small business in south-central Los Angeles, who look me in my eye and say, "Your lifestyle is unacceptable."

"Unacceptable?" That's not a word you hear much in this

country. Unacceptable? We've moved all of the rules. I can do whatever I want to any time I want to. The femi-

STAR PARKER is president and founder of the Coalition on Urban Renewal and Education and author of *Pimps, Whores and Welfare Brats*. Prior to her conservative activism, she was a single welfare mother in Los Angeles. She reformed her life, received a degree in marketing, and launched an urban Christian magazine. She lives in Southern California with her two daughters.

nists said I belonged to myself. The leaders that represent me, because they wear the same color skin I do, told me that America is inherently racist so I don't have to mainstream. On and on and on I could go with the relativism that is plaguing our nation, and they said, "You can believe all the lies of the Left if you want to, but your lifestyle is unacceptable to God."

And I tell you, when I heard that word "God," I felt guilty. I didn't know any Baptists, but I knew that they like that guilt thing and I thought maybe these guys are Baptist and I thought let me get out of here.

And I got out of there as quickly as I could. But they kept calling me. I'd already filled out the application to get a little job. I wanted some under the table money because, remember, the laws of the old welfare state: don't work, don't save, and don't get married and we'll keep sending you a check.

But, they kept calling me. If I'd known a lawyer from the ACLU, I could have sued them for religious harassment. But because I didn't, I ended up in church with them, and shook my head yes when the preacher said, "Do you want to get saved?"— it was my custom, saying yes. I mean, anyone that can break and enter into someone's house because someone asked them to, or commit armed robbery because someone asked them to, surely when they walk in the door and someone says, "Would you like some real peace?" I could say yes.

It didn't take long for me to think about the difference between the misery I had and God, Creator of heaven and earth—you know, the God they try to remove from everywhere in society. Maybe if we steal the symbols out of society, we can get rid of Him altogether. But there are certain aspects of God they just cannot get rid of. He's just there, and we know it, like every time we fly, and we get up over those bumpy clouds, and we see His presence above them.

> One day, I had a gut instinct way down deep that there was something wrong with killing your offspring.

So I'm thinking about that God, and comparing him to this $430 and a few goodies a month, and the next day I wrote my caseworker and told her, take my name off; I'm going with the Lord.

It wasn't that easy, you know. The miracles didn't start happening overnight. I had to straighten myself up, go out there, and get a job to support my little daughter.

We don't think about how hard it is for these girls in housing projects across this nation to walk into a corporate structure and try to get the job we've asked them to do. I'd been told for over twenty-five years that white people don't hire blacks. I had to walk into that particular situation, and good thing the guy in there was a little-bitty white guy, because I figured, if he doesn't hire me, I'll just beat him up.

But he hired me. Gave me an opportunity to find out that God was in the talent distribution business. Because I was sitting there, answering telephones in a food distribution company selling salt and pepper over the telephone. And I did it with joy. You know, Scripture says, the joy of the Lord. So I'm sitting there with joy.

This little-bitty white guy named Tom walked by my desk one day and said, "You sure talk a lot. Have you ever considered sales and marketing?" And to make a long story short, I found out talking was my talent.

During the 1992 Los Angeles riots, I saw the dream of my business go up in flames, not because my personal structure got burned down, but because the advertisers in this little magazine I started got burned out. But God used that to focus me on cultural renewal and welfare reform. That's about when I linked up with The Heritage Foundation and Young America's Foundation and said to myself, "You know what? There's something you can contribute here."

So now I talk not only in housing projects, but on national television. It's interesting to be able to work in all of these arenas, to talk about welfare reform, and how it impacted our nation negatively, particularly the black family. Prior to Johnson's experiment, we started seeing consistency in the rise of black marriages, despite the Great Depression, a couple of world wars, and all types of other obstacles such as Jim Crow laws and forced segregation.

Yet those people managed to maintain their homes; as late as 1965, 78 percent of black husbands were in their homes with their families, despite racism and poverty. Then came the Great Society, and the illegitimacy rates in black America soared to 70 percent.

Those against organizations like ours have said, "Oh, that's somebody else's fault. That's because of racism. That's because of poverty."

And we said, "Wait a minute. Let's look at poverty: 28 percent of poor people in the nation today are black; 32 percent are Hispanic; 8 percent are white. You know, there's a little problem here in terms of race."

> Remember, the laws of the old welfare state: don't work, don't save, and don't get married and we'll keep sending you a check.

And we can say, "But these charts also show that 70 percent of poor people have something else in common: they're single, and trying to raise children by themselves."

Generally, I find a lot of my problems in two places: selling these ideas in black America, even through the church; and selling them on campuses. These campuses are vicious. Just this week I was at the University of Denver and the students had been fired up by the Gay and Lesbian Associations, and the Multiculturalists, and the Black Student Union this, and Every Kind of Group that. These people have plagued our colleges with the politics of guilt and pity. They come in with their hidden agenda, propagandize these kids, and take their entire biblical worldview from them. But I am happy to be there because I can just point my finger in the faces of the enemy and tell them how destructive their agenda is.

Appearances at women's colleges are very good. I remember when I went to Hillary Clinton's alma mater, Wellesley, you could hear a pin drop. You'd think we were at a Catholic Church. A little lady got up and she's telling them how wonderful liberalism is. And then it was my time, and I got up and said, "You know, radical feminism has created the environment that has allowed illegitimacy and poverty to skyrocket." And the place went dead quiet. Even in the question and answer time, there was, like, nothing.

Not only are we contending with the agenda of the Left on these campuses—feminism, the black student unions who insist that America is inherently racist, and the multicultural agenda—but also with the aggression of the homosexual movement. It's just amazing how they plague these colleges: they make it very, very difficult just to express an opinion publicly.

That's what we want—just to express our opinion. We want to offer another idea, to say, "Let people choose for themselves." The reason I got involved in this whole social policy arena is because I wanted to tell the people that were in the same situation I had been in—living in the heart of the inner city, thinking there's no hope for me, but I know there's a better way— that yes, there is: God loves you.

I just want to tell them about the Gospel. God's not mad at you. He'll take care of you. And I found out that I couldn't do it without Him.

You can't go into the schools. Nope, they belong to the state. And they'll tell you who comes in, and with what message. We can't go into the welfare services, either. You will not believe how much paperwork and bureaucracy stands in the way of just being able to talk in housing projects. I thought it was public property.

So I ended up bringing my little self out here to

Washington, D.C., because I found out that's where the real laws come from. And if the Lord hands me out the penance to run for a public office and I make the ultimate sacrifice, I warn you, it'll be for one term only. Because I am not going to shut up. I have my one talent, and you can forget it.

> Good thing the guy in there was a little-bitty white guy, because I figured, if he doesn't hire me, I'll just beat him up.

We have a tremendous amount of work to do, because the polls show that we haven't sold our message, we haven't begun to dismantle some of the madness of the last forty years; it has become too entrenched. How do you eat a cow? One little t-bone steak at a time.

I can yak all day, but I want to leave you with three ways we can work on various issues, because issues of race and poverty in this country are not going to go away. In fact, after we began this war on poverty, we started to see an escalation of tension in the racial arena.

I like the way that Michael Baumann, a professor at Hillsdale, said it when he was talking about the attitudes that we have to contend with when we're attempting to change people from depending on government to depending on themselves. He said that if a poor man believes that the wealthy are thieves who exploit others, the poor man is not going to emulate that man and take the necessary steps to get out of poverty.

And we all know the steps out of poverty. The first step is to understand that I have an obligation—self-government's first step. I have an obligation to be self-sufficient and to make proper choices. It's my obligation to my neighbor, to society. There is no responsibility in welfare; it is somebody else's fault, I'm entitled to these benefits.

And you cannot understand morality without God. Today we could have 270 million people out there determining for themselves what right and wrong is—like that young man down in San Diego who fired on his classmates. He didn't think he did anything wrong.

We don't make up the rules for art. We don't make up the rules for science. We learn them. Well, God has laws too, and guidelines. You had better know the rules in order to live a successful life of self-governing. And if you can't, then you are going to end up with a martial state, because somebody's got to call the shots and say what right and wrong is. So it's either God's law, or the government's law.

The second step out of poverty is to understand that you need additional training. You have to learn as you go through life. That's why Republican is better for me, because in the area of training and education, Republicans say, "You've got to learn. You're going to have to learn how to read, how to write, how to do math. You're going to have to learn how to think critically.

"We don't care how you do that. Go to a charter school, go to a home school, go to a public school, go to a private school, go to a parochial school, just do it, okay?"

The Democrats? What do they say? "We know how you're

going to learn. So we have this one size fits all program. We're going to tie the teachers hands behind their back with government regulations."

The teachers look out at their classrooms and say, "You, you're special ed. I can tell by the color of your skin. Go down the hallway. You, you speak another language in your home so you're going down there and get some bilingual studies, because man, it's going to mean a whole lot more money for our school district." A bigger group of whites get Ritalin. The few who are left are taught how to tolerate all the ones they just sent out of the classroom.

My daughter went to this little government school that didn't have enough books for the kids, or lockers either. They didn't have enough money. I didn't know then that she was worth almost $7,000 to them, just the one little kid. With $7,000 I would have home schooled her. They didn't have enough money for that, but they were debating condom distribution machines. And they had enough money for a soda machine for seventh graders.

Next step out of poverty. Developing a work ethic. The third step out of poverty is to work. That's why it was beautiful to put the work ethic in the welfare bill.

We need healthy households, you know, husband, wife, and kids. Not to need a man is a feminist line. Kids need them. Because men do more than bring their paycheck home. They teach girls modesty, just by being around. And they teach the boys the work ethic.

The next step out of poverty is to save and invest. That's why I'm working now on Social Security privatization—I'm supposed to call it "personalizing" Social Security. Personal retirement accounts. Save and invest.

The Bible says a good man leaves an inheritance to his grandchildren. People that make $73,000 or more can do that more readily, because whatever the government doesn't pay for, they can put into an account. People in the middle can squeeze a little bit and get a little bit in a 401(k) or a personal IRA.

But people on the bottom, the little bit that they could save, is being forced into a black hole: 6.2 percent out of their check, 6.2 percent out of their employer's check. They can't transfer, and they get a horrible rate of return.

The fifth and final step out of poverty is sexual restraint—marriage before children. And that's going to take some doing. We must all work very aggressively to get some abstinence educational curriculum into the schools and make sure that children at a young age understand how to make proper decisions for their lives, not live a life of despair and poverty.

But we must also, at the grassroots level, make sure that when children find themselves in a crisis that they have somewhere to go other than the Department of Social Services. If, for example, they have a drug problem, they should be able to go to the twelve-step program at the local church. That goes for help with pregnancies too.

The place not to go to is Planned Parenthood. There are good maternity homes for the expectant mother that also place the child for adoption into a wonderful family if that is the mother's choice. And they can assist the mother to get back on track.

It's time to start building again, because the days of welfare are over. While we're dismantling, we need to make sure that people are built up.

I like to share my story because I'm a living witness that the things that we talk about here in Washington, D.C., and many of you are working on, do work. The ideas are very, very beautiful, because they're out of our control.

It's something that God has already done. He loves each and every person that He has created, and He has given each and every one of us a unique role in life. Part of it is to be healthy individuals, which make up healthy households, which then make up healthy neighborhoods. And healthy neighborhoods make up healthy communities, healthy cities, healthy states, and finally a healthy nation. Under God. ■

I COULDN'T EXPLAIN WHY,
BUT FROM THE MOMENT
OF MY ABORTION, I HAD
THIS LONGING TO HOLD MY
CHILD.

—CARMEN PATE

FROM PRO-CHOICE
TO LIFE: *One Mother's Story*

BY CARMEN PATE
WASHINGTON, D.C., JULY 9, 1999
EXCERPTS FROM A SPEECH AT THE CONSERVATIVE WOMEN'S NETWORK

MUCH IS BEING SAID ABOUT our culture, particularly since the shooting at Columbine High School. Many are asking, What's wrong with our culture? Who's to blame? Who can fix it? Or even, Is it too late to be fixed? When the shooting occurred I began to reflect on my own life, where I'd been and where I hoped to go, and my mind went to some comments of Lon Solomon, senior pastor at McLean Bible Church. Recently Pastor Solomon talked about his past, a past filled with drugs, free sex, and pagan gods. And he said, "My idea of a perfect world was one where drugs would be legalized, where sex would have no restrictions, and where abortion would be legal." Then he said, "You know, it wasn't a piece of legislation or a law that changed my heart, but a confrontation with God himself." And, he added, "That's the way we're going to change the culture; we're going to change hearts, one heart at a time."

Just last evening, I had the opportunity to attend a fund-raising banquet

CARMEN PATE most recently served as president of Concerned Women of America. She was also the executive director of a crisis pregnancy center in Texas and executive director of the End Hunger Network in Houston. The mother of three grown children, she lives with her husband, in Virginia.

for a project that's being started in D.C.'s inner city, Anacostia. It's called, "The House." The project is being coordinated by two former NFL players, Ricky Bolton and Steve Fitshugh of the Denver Broncos. They were passionately concerned about the people in the inner city, particularly the children, and the teenagers. They said that government programs hadn't worked; more police and more drug programs hadn't worked either. What these kids needed were people willing to give of themselves, to build relationships with them. And, in doing so, introducing them to God, who also loves them. That way you change one heart at a time, and show them the truth of God's love.

Lon Solomon had other words of wisdom when he answered the question: "How many psychologists does it take to change a light bulb?" He said, "It only takes one, but the light bulb has to want to change." Because, it comes down to human nature, people have to want to change. We have to touch their hearts first. We have to be able to reach out to people where they are before they will even begin to listen to the truth that we have to tell them.

I can relate to change that takes place in the heart. You see, I, too, came from the other side. For about ten years of my life, I wore the pro-choice label and I was very proud of it. I was out there on the front lines, fighting for women's abortion rights—just as passionate about that side as I am about the life side today. But you see, I never bothered to really check out the truth. I was certain that all the things that I would claim about abortion must be true. Looking back, I realize that the reason I was so gullible was because I feared the truth. Because, if I were to determine what the truth was about abortion and about life, I would have to admit that I may have made a mistake. You see, I aborted two of my children.

It still hurts when I think about my past choices. I was already a single mom, and we all know how difficult that can be, don't we? And I was on a career path that would mean more money and ultimate success. You couldn't expect me to give up all of that, could you? Wouldn't an abortion be more liberating for me? Besides, those earliest stages of gestation, we're only talking about a lot of tissue anyway, right? Isn't that right? You see, I so wanted to believe that those things were true, that motherhood was distressing, that abortion was liberating, and that the baby was just a ball of tissue.

But something else was happening inside of me. I couldn't explain why, but from the moment of my abortion, I had this longing to hold my child. But when I would mention it to my feminist friends, they would say, oh, no, that's not what you're feeling. And I would say, but how would you explain the nightmares of my body being dismembered and someone wanting to kill me? Oh, it's not the abortion, they would say, it's just those pro-life people trying to make you feel guilty about what you've done.

I didn't understand the physical complications, the depression. I didn't understand the breakdown in my fellowship with God. No one had told me that abortion wasn't really liberating. No one had ever told me that the relationship between a mother and a baby begins at conception, and that when the relationship is severed, it can never be brought back. A mother feels a void that is there forever. Even when she has gone through counseling and been healed and restored, the void is still there.

When I realized that all these things were happening to me I cried out and said, "Oh, God, I want to know the truth." Well, as only God can do, He listens and He does give second chances. And He opens our eyes to the truth if we allow Him to do so. It was amazing, I began to get information from people and friends, and I did some research in the library. Then when I saw the sonogram of a friend's ten-week-old-baby, in uterus, I knew, finally, that we were talking about a child.

When a woman has finally learned the truth she must speak up and say, "No more!" We must make sure that the sanctity of life is once again respected—not only for the sake of the child, but for ourselves. I made a commitment to God that I would make sure, with all the power that He gives me, that women know the truth about abortion, so that they will not be exploited by lies as I was.

There have been an estimated 40 million abortions since *Roe v. Wade*. A survey of post-abortive women conducted by a group called Women Exploited by Abortion leads me to believe that at least 25 million women who have had abortions have been traumatized. And many of those women are silent. Why? One reason is because our society has made it politically incorrect to say that you're suffering from the symptoms of post-abortion syndrome, and yet, we know they are real, very, very real. Thousands of women have testified that post-abortion syndrome does exist and lasts a lifetime, affecting a woman's entire family. We were victims.

> No one had ever told me that the relationship between a mother and a baby begins at conception, and that when the relationship is severed, it can never be brought back. A mother feels a void that is there forever.

Well, we have come together. David Reardon wrote a book some years ago called, *Aborted Women: Silent No More.* A class action lawsuit was filed in New Jersey by three post-abortive women, and two female obstetricians, who contended that, in fact, women have been exploited by abortion. Their right to informed consent was denied. How can that be, if a woman says she wants to have an abortion and signs the form? Well, think of adoption. Many states today have adoption laws stating that a woman cannot give informed consent to release her baby for adoption until she has held the baby in her arms because the maternal relationship is real. Therefore, until she has held the baby, consent is not informed. The maternal instinct says I have a baby inside of me that is part of who I am. And man cannot sever that relationship. This lawsuit says we must recognize what science and what medical history have told us for years—that life does begin at conception. There's simply no doubt about it.

Roe v. Wade became law in our country in 1973. Opponents

to abortion said it didn't have a legal leg to stand on. But it seems that no one was willing to challenge it, until now, until this fabulous case, *Donna Santa Marie v. Christine Todd Whitman*, state of New Jersey. The exciting news is that we are mobilizing post-abortive women across the country; we hope to get one million friends of the court in this lawsuit. As the word gets out, through the Internet and meetings and gatherings in churches, the names come pouring in, women saying yes, I'm suffering from post-abortion syndrome and I don't want it to happen to anyone else. It's about changing hearts, about letting mothers be proud that they can be mothers. It's allowing that child who has never had anyone to stand up for him or her say, "I have rights, too, from the womb, because I am a person."

Needless to say, the abortion industry will be fighting every step of the way because abortion is a multibillion-dollar business. One of the members of our task force is Carol Everett, a former abortionist out of Dallas, Texas. She ran several abortion clinics and she talks about the grief, about what she calls the blood money.

It's time for abortions to stop. And we can do it. We can change the culture in America. It's going to take all of us through the legislative channel but also by changing one heart at a time. I pray that you will be bold in standing up and fighting against the greatest human rights abuse that ever existed, the one against women and children—abortion. ■

I F YOU DON'T COMMUNI-
CATE THE MESSAGE AND
YOU DON'T LEARN TO
DELIVER IT WELL, WHAT'S THE
POINT OF HAVING A MESSAGE?
AND WE HAVE A MESSAGE OF
TRUTH.

—RANDALL BROOKS PHILLIPS

FROM THE BROADWAY STAGE TO THE POLITICAL STAGE

What Annie Taught Me
About Being a Good Conservative

RANDALL BROOKS PHILLIPS
WASHINGTON, D.C., JULY 21, 2000
EXCERPTS FROM A SPEECH AT THE CONSERVATIVE WOMEN'S NETWORK

I SUSPECT YOU ALL REMEMBER *ANNIE*, right? Well, I believe that Annie was a conservative. After all, Annie was the victim of a poorly run government agency, an orphanage. And the director of that orphanage, no matter how rotten, couldn't be fired from her government job. In any case, what I learned on stage taught me the very basic tenets of conservatism.

First and foremost is responsibility. As you know, I'm sure, one of the biggest problems in our society is that nobody wants to take responsibility for anything. If you fail at school, you blame it on repressed memory syndrome. If you can't keep a job, your mother looked at you cross-eyed when you were a baby. If you get pregnant out of wedlock, your teacher didn't teach you how to use a condom. But my family

As a child, **RANDALL PHILLIPS** appeared in over 640 performances on Broadway in the hit musical *Annie*. After serving as Capitol Hill and White House correspondent for CBN News, she founded Spectrum Media, a media strategist and public relations firm. She lives in Virginia with her husband, Tom, and son, Reagan.

taught me responsibility. That's probably what made me such a good cast member—I was responsible.

Seven children and one dog basically held the fate of the multimillion dollar production *Annie* on their very small shoulders, eight shows a week. If any one of the seven kids decided that he or she just didn't feel like going on stage that day, that's it, you're out. It didn't matter how tired, how sick, or how bored you were. The show must go on, as they say. To learn that kind of responsibility at such a young age prepared me well for future challenges.

While I was playing an orphan and also serving as understudy to Annie, the girl playing the title role bumped her mouth with a prop early on in the show and ran off stage. Without really thinking, I looked down at the orchestra leader in the pit. We locked eyes, and he mouthed the word, "Sing." And I sang. I took over the role of Annie, although I had never even had an understudy rehearsal.

All I wanted to do at the end of the show, despite the standing ovation, was to take a nap. But instead I had to give a press conference. A reporter asked me how I was able to think so clearly, to take over like that at such a young age. And I said, totally innocently, "The fact that I wasn't on drugs had a lot to do with it." And it was true; children as young as seven were being offered drugs backstage by crewmembers, who apparently thought it was funny. (My parents threatened to take me out of the show if things didn't improve backstage.)

But this was not my first exposure to the effects of drug

abuse. Before *Annie*, I was a child model for Ann Klein. And I remember one particular designer who would kneel in front of me, pulling and pinning and pinching, and over time, I saw this man's nose falling off of his face from cocaine abuse. Imagine asking, at ten years of age, "Mommy, why is that man's nose falling off?"

After I left Broadway, because I had been outspoken about the horrors of drugs, I was asked to work with a nationwide antidrug campaign run by Art Linkletter. And someone from the Reagan/Bush campaign heard me and said, "You ought to get this kid on the celebrity surrogates roster." So I started out, primarily singing "Tomorrow," which is a song of hope that expressed Reagan's vision for America after the malaise of the Carter years.

Some of you may recall that during a debate in Ohio, Carter said he often discussed foreign policy with his daughter, Amy, at which everyone in the audience laughed. It became a national joke. Overnight, the press traveling with our group decided that this "Annie" kid must be Reagan's answer to Amy Carter. So a reporter asked me what I thought about Carter's policy on the Panama Canal. Well, the campaign staff literally held their breath. But, fortunately, I was born in Panama. And being a good conservative and raised as such, I had a definite and well-informed opinion on the Panama Canal. Which again, fortunately, was right in line with Reagan's. The next thing I knew I was out on the road speaking about numerous political issues. They even gave me a title, National Honorary Chairman of Youth for Reagan/Bush.

So it was only natural that the two threads of my life—the performing thread and the politics thread—would come together at some point and lead me to a new role in the media field for a total of nine years, seven at CBN, and now as a media consultant and coach. I truly believe that everything that I learned on that Broadway stage prepared me to do the variety of things that I've done since. Most of which involved being thrown into situations without really being prepared, having to take charge, take responsibility, and forge ahead.

I would like to talk briefly about three of the lessons that I've learned from Broadway, in addition to responsibility. These three lessons will help explain how that experience taught me to be a better conservative, and how we might all become better conservatives if we do heed this advice.

First, when you're in a Broadway show, some performers may have more responsibility than others, but whether it's a small part or a leading role, you're all part of the same cast. You're part of the same team. And if one cast member deviates from the script, the whole show suffers. Every performer wants to have his or her moment in the sun, but the minute you start thinking about upstaging someone else, even subconsciously, the very fabric of the show changes.

It's a good lesson for conservatives, for we don't often play by these rules. We all have issues and candidates and causes that we consider more important than others, but once we become members of the same team, we have to read from the same script. The Democrats and liberals are very good at this, but we conservatives fail at it time and time again.

I'm one of the strongest advocates of school choice. At CBN, covering this issue, it became a real passion. But I wouldn't boycott a convention if all of a sudden the nominee should say, "You know, I've changed my mind. I don't support school choice."

> **If you can't make them listen, nobody will know how good the message is. And if they don't know how good it is, what's the point?**

As I mentioned earlier, the show must go on. The audience doesn't much care if you don't feel like going on stage one night. They're there to be entertained. In politics, sometimes our particular issues don't get as much attention as we might like, but our audience is the American electorate and they don't much care what went on before the curtain went up. What they need is to be led and to be inspired. We can't do that as a party or a movement if one or more of our cast members carries baggage on stage with them.

The second lesson is related to the first. Don't engage in political cannibalism. In *Annie*, we went through many different cast members, when one or more actors left the show. And some actors didn't quite live up to the original portrayal of certain characters. Everybody knew it. One adult character, in particular, just wasn't quite as good as the original actress. It wasn't that her portrayal was bad, it just wasn't quite as good. But those of us who worked with the original actress didn't bad-mouth the new cast member publicly. We would never do that. But we *do* eat our own in the conservative movement and in the Republican Party. I'd love to see somebody like Alan Keyes or Chris Cox have a shot at the nomination for president someday. But they're not our candidates now. And the disappointment that your candidate didn't win shouldn't linger to the extent of bad-mouthing the candidate who did win. The Democrats and the liberals don't do that. Neither should we.

Remember, no one new will come to our show if we give ourselves bad reviews. All that does is turn off the audience and give the media more ammunition with which to shoot us down. The Democrats don't do this, and that is why they have a better record of recruitment.

The last lesson that I learned on Broadway that makes me a better conservative is this: Know your audience. When you do almost seven hundred shows, you learn that every audience is different. Sometimes they laugh at exactly the same place in the script, sometimes the laugh is delayed, sometimes they don't laugh at all. What's funny or scary or a chuckle to a certain group of people may not be the same to another group of people. As an actor or an actress, you'll learn to pick up on these subtle things. And you adjust your performance accordingly. I'm not talking about straying from the script, but how you "play the script." There's nothing quite so wonderful as tuning in to an audience, having them in the palm of your hand, being able to move them this way or that way.

It's not the acting per se. It's the ability to sway people to the way you believe. Conservatives tend to have a little problem with this. We don't know how to play to different audiences. Those of us who do know often get shot down by people who say that the message itself ought to be enough, that it doesn't need to be articulated well. But if you can't make them listen, nobody will know how good the message is. And if they don't know how good it is, what's the point?

> **The great thing is that our message is the truth. We shouldn't be ashamed of packaging our message.**

As a whole, conservatives make two obvious mistakes. We get so depressed about the media portraying us unfairly and bungling our message that we either give up trying to market it, or we tend to think that it will sell itself. But that doesn't work in politics, or on Broadway. The lines are just lines on a script until they're acted. The same thing is true with our message. Until it's lived and believed and articulated, it's just a message.

But there are people in our movement, and you will encounter them, who think that packaging and marketing our conservative message corrupts the message. Well, they're wrong. You know the Folger's coffee commercial where the woman gets out of bed in the morning and does an Irish Lord of Dance kind of jig? Coffee doesn't do that for me, but I keep hoping it will, because I've seen the commercial, and I'm sold on Folger's. I'm also terrified of flying. But when I do fly, I fly United. You know why? Because they have friendlier skies. They do, I'm convinced of it.

Democrats know all of this because they have accepted what good advertisers have learned through research. Americans love a pitch. But we conservatives don't seem to understand this.

During the Reagan campaign days, there were a whole series of buttons: Lithuanians for Reagan; Serbs and Croatians for Reagan; Azerbajanians for Reagan. The public relations and marketing point was that Americans like to feel as if you're talking to them specifically, and we conservatives don't do that. The great thing is that our message is the truth. We shouldn't be ashamed of packaging our message and getting to know our different audiences. It's the other side that ought to be ashamed for trying to sell the American electorate a lie.

Still, many in our movement disagree loudly and we have to make those dissenters understand that we'll never compete successfully against the liberal philosophy, whether in college campuses or the kindergarten level, in film or stage or book, if we don't compete in the marketing game.

If you don't communicate the message and you don't learn to deliver it well, what's the point of having a message? And we have a message of truth.

Once again, the three lessons I learned from Broadway. First, let's all pull together and be good cast mates even though we may have had previous disagreements. Second, let's encourage and inspire our American political audience—the voters—to follow us, not just tell them that the show would have been better with a different cast and expect them to show up at the ballot box and vote for us anyway. Third, let's allow the "rightness" of our message to shine in any light and *create* the light that shines on it, not just accept the way the media and detractors shine a light on us. We won't win just by being right. Only if we do these three things will we experience what I experienced on a Broadway stage, and that is the intoxication and the satisfaction of reaching the very last person in the very last row and giving them not only the hope of a brighter tomorrow but of a better America. ■

BILL CLINTON'S CHIEF FOREIGN POLICY ADVISOR, STROBE TALBOT, WROTE IN *Time* MAGAZINE, "NATIONHOOD AS WE KNOW IT WILL BE OBSOLETE; ALL STATES WILL RECOGNIZE A SINGLE GLOBAL AUTHORITY."

—PHYLLIS SCHLAFLY

The Legacy of Clinton's Web of Treaties

BY PHYLLIS SCHLAFLY
WASHINGTON, D.C., MAY 4, 2001
EXCERPTS FROM A SPEECH AT THE CONSERVATIVE WOMEN'S NETWORK

BILL CLINTON IS GONE from the White House but his legacy lives on, and this legacy is not merely his contemptible treatment of women. His legacy is his web of treaties, the progeny of the UN conferences he participated in, his executive orders, and his international engagements.

Clinton made no secret about what he was for. He went before the UN General Assembly in 1997 and proclaimed a "new global era" and an "emerging international system." He used a very apt metaphor. He said he was taking America into a "web" of institutions and arrangements to set the international ground rules for the twenty-first century. He went on to say that "the forces of global integration are a great tide, inexorably wearing away the established order of things." He described our troops lost in a helicopter crash in Bosnia as "citizens of the world." The following month, Bill Clinton went down to Argentina and said he was trying to promote a "reorganization of the

PHYLLIS SCHLAFLY is president and founder of Eagle Forum. She is a lawyer, syndicated columnist, talk radio host, and author and editor of sixteen books. From 1972 to 1982, she led a successful campaign against the feminists' Equal Rights Amendment. The mother of six grown children, she lives in St. Louis.

world" into a global system by merging "integrated economies and integrated democracies."

The American people never signed off on "integrating" our economy with corrupt, bankrupt regimes where people work for wages of 25 and 50 cents an hour. And the American people certainly don't want to "integrate" our republic with totalitarian countries where people have no constitutional rights. Bill Clinton surrounded himself with people who wanted to do exactly this. His chief foreign policy advisor was Strobe Talbot, his Rhodes scholar and draft-dodging buddy who wrote in *Time* magazine, "Nationhood as we know it will be obsolete; all states will recognize a single global authority."

That's what these people were trying to bring about—not, of course, with one fell swoop because the American people would never accept that, but one step at a time through treaties, international conferences, executive orders, and the assignments of our armed services.

The worst of all these treaties was the International Criminal Court Treaty that Clinton signed on New Year's Eve. For the first time, it would give a foreign court the authority to try individuals, not just nations as the World Court does. The crimes have not yet been defined, but we do know there will be no Bill of Rights. This treaty puts all American service men and women at risk all over the world, and probably American travelers, too. Although this treaty was not ratified by the Senate, this impudent bunch of foreigners in The Hague is trying to assert the authority of the

International Criminal Court over the United States anyway.

Another treaty that is dear to the hearts of both Bill and Hillary Clinton is the United Nations Convention on the Rights of the Child. It would set up a whole series of "rights" that the child could assert against his parents, as, for example, the right to rest and leisure. What in the world does that mean? You discipline your child for sassing you at the dinner table and the child says, "I have my UN right to express myself freely."

This does not conform with American understanding of law at all. But all of these treaties, every one of them, sets up some kind of committee of so-called experts who will monitor compliance.

Another treaty dear to the hearts of Bill and Hillary Clinton is the UN Treaty on the Elimination of All Forms of Discrimination Against Women. This would give us an international equal rights amendment enforced by a committee of foreign experts. At one point, Clinton held a gathering in the Rose Garden with all his favorite feminists and announced that he was terribly embarrassed that we had not yet ratified this treaty. It is curious the sort of things that embarrass President Clinton.

They say old soldiers never die, they just fade away, but I can tell you, old treaties never die, they don't even fade away. They stay in the bottom drawer and can be called up for ratification at any time. This web of treaties is part of Clinton's major legacy.

Another principle one is the Global Warming Treaty, now called the Kyoto Protocol. We call it the hot air treaty. It comes out of the extreme environmental ideas in Al Gore's book, *Earth in the Balance.* This treaty is an attempt to regulate our economic life. It would bind the United States to reduce our energy emissions to 7 percent below our 1990 level. Energy is the basis of our high standard of living. Such a reduction would cost a million jobs and massive disruptions in our economy. These drastic cutbacks would be enforced by big tax increases on gasoline, home fuel, and electricity. Meanwhile, under the terms of the treaty, China, India, Mexico, and a hundred other developing nations would have no limitations at all.

All this is based on the junk science about global warming and predictions that are no more reliable than the weatherman's guess of how much snow will fall in the next twenty years. The influence of this unratified treaty can already be noted in the new regulations to limit the use of energy in washing machines. Clinton issued these regulations based on the fear of global warming. As a result, the new machines will cost from about $240 to $500 more than the current models.

Clinton also tried to revive the Law of the Sea Treaty, which Ronald Reagan killed when he was president. This treaty would force American businesses to spend billions of dollars to bring up the riches on the ocean floor and then turn them over to an international authority to distribute to Third World countries.

UN treaties to control the environment and take over the management of large areas of American land started with the Earth Summit in Rio in 1972. Fortunately, the first President Bush refused to sign the Biodiversity Treaty. When Clinton became president, Al Gore persuaded him to sign it. The Senate, however, refused to ratify it. But Clinton's legacy lives on. All sorts of fallout from this unratified treaty continue to plague us. For example, Clinton's executive order called the American Heritage Rivers Initiative enabled him to take over ten rivers last year, putting hundreds of thousands of acres along their banks under the control of federal regulators. This is a direct attack on personal property rights.

Clinton's executive order called the American Heritage Rivers Initiative enabled him to take over ten rivers last year, putting hundreds of thousands of acres along their banks under the control of federal regulators. This is a direct attack on personal property rights.

Another result of the 1972 Earth Summit is Clinton's Council on Sustainable Development. We have a law against the federal government writing curriculum for the public schools, but the Clinton administration ignored it. This council has issued all sorts of curricula on environmental education for the public schools. The message of these curricula is to make kids feel guilty that the United States uses more energy per person than any other country in the world.

These UN conferences cause all kinds of mischief. At one conference, these overpaid UN bureaucrats got together and thought up a nifty idea that is now being promoted as the Tobin Tax. This would enable the UN to tax all international currency transactions, providing an independent source of revenue so the United Nations would not have to worry about whether the U.S. Congress passes the appropriations or not.

The UN Millennium Assembly was another UN conference. It convened in New York last September and produced a whole list of mischievous ideas, the worst of which were to establish a United Nations army, start an international registry of private gun ownership, and minimize the influence of America in the United Nations by abolishing our veto and our permanent membership on the Security Council. Those things have not come about, but the UN bureaucrats are working on them.

I hope you noticed that the United States has been kicked off of the UN Human Rights Commission. Space was made for countries that don't respect human rights, such as Sudan, Libya, Uganda, Cuba, and China.

Another of the treaties that Clinton locked us into was the World Trade Organization. It was sold to us as free trade, but is actually trade managed by a bunch of bureaucrats in Geneva. The World Trade Organization has a legislature of 135 countries including Haiti and Cuba. The WTO judicial process produces decisions made in secret, and from which there is no appeal. The WTO has already ruled against the United States four times.

In this sorry tale about treaties, we had one victory. We did defeat the Nuclear Test Ban Treaty. This was very important for the defense of our country, and the defeat was a big shock to the Clintonites.

Another treaty that Clinton got the Senate to ratify was the NATO Expansion Treaty, which commits us to defend the borders of countries in Eastern Europe, borders that people have been fighting about for thousands of years. There isn't any legal connection between the NATO Expansion Treaty and our engagements in Bosnia and Yugoslavia, but there is a psychological link. Madeleine Albright made it clear, when Clinton started his unconstitutional war in Yugoslavia, that we had to relinquish some of our sovereignty to NATO.

> Ronald Reagan's military vision was firmly grounded in the principle of peace through strength The Clinton policy was exactly the opposite—use our superb military for any purpose the administration might think advantageous at the time.

NATO is used in order to make an end run around national sovereignty. One of the purposes is to avoid the constitutional requirement that only Congress can declare war. It's obvious that there was never any exit plan to bring U.S. troops home from either Bosnia or Yugoslavia.

As for Yugoslavia, NATO now seems to be changing sides. Clinton's bombing was started in order to get the Serbs out of Kosovo. Well, we got the Serbs out of Kosovo, and now we find that the people we turned Kosovo over to are worse than the Serbs. The cutthroat Albanians are now trying to move into Macedonia.

Ronald Reagan's military vision was firmly grounded in the

principle of peace through strength—that America should have more power than any other country so that the bad guys won't push us around. The Clinton policy was exactly the opposite—use our superb military for any purpose the administration might think advantageous at the time.

We must address one more area of Clinton's legacy: his executive orders. His Presidential Decision Directive 25 (PDD25) purported to give the president the authority to place U.S. forces under the operational control of a foreign commander and under the United Nations rules of engagement. PDD25 has never been rescinded.

Clinton also issued an executive order to try to lock us into the defunct and obsolete 1972 ABM Treaty. Fortunately, President George W. Bush believes it is out of date and that we should no longer comply with it.

We're still dealing with Clinton's outrageous executive order that purports to make *not* speaking English a new civil right. He ordered all federal agencies to provide federal benefits in languages other than English. Four days before Janet Reno left office, she issued fifteen pages of regulations to implement this executive order. This and subsequent regulations issued by other executive branch departments were based on a lower court decision called *Alexander vs. Sandoval,* which has now been reversed by the U.S. Supreme Court.

This Supreme Court decision offers one of the most significant opportunities for conservatives in years, and we should take advantage of it immediately. It has had almost no press coverage. The Department of Health and Human Services is trying to force doctors to hire translators in case any Medicaid or Medicare patient might not speak English. We should immediately move to make sure that our government speaks to us only in our national language, which is English. The English language is important to the maintenance of support for the U.S. Constitution and Declaration of Independence. It is particularly important to conservatives because many terms used by conservatives cannot be accurately translated into other languages: conservative, limited government, due process, separation of powers, states' rights.

Clinton's legacy lives on through UN treaties, UN conferences, and Clinton's executive orders. They constitute a real threat to our way of life, to our energy consumption, to our standard of living, and to the Constitution itself. George Washington warned us in his Farewell Address to steer clear of permanent alliances with any foreign country. It is time to heed his words: Let us raise a standard to which the wise and honest can repair. The event is in the hands of God. ■

THE ONCE VALIANT WOMEN'S MOVEMENT THAT I EMBRACED IS NO LONGER ABOUT FAIRNESS, EQUALITY, OPPORTUNITY, AND RESPECT FOR ALL WOMEN—IT'S ABOUT THE POLITICS OF SELEC- TIVE DIVERSITY AND, ULTIMATE- LY, OF DIVISIVENESS. IT IS ANTI- FEMALE, ANTI-FAMILY, AND ANTI- CHILDREN.

—DR. LAURA SCHLESSINGER

AUTHENTIC FEMINISM

BY DR. LAURA SCHLESSINGER
WASHINGTON, D.C., JUNE 5, 2001
EXCERPTS FROM A SPEECH AT THE CONSERVATIVE WOMEN'S NETWORK

IN MY NEVER-TO-BE-HUMBLE OPINION, by now—I'm fifty-four years old—the feminist movement should have made me its patron saint. I mean, here I am, a woman, in the top tier of the seriously male-dominated world of talk radio—and I'm internationally syndicated. Seven years ago, although I had the biggest share of any talk show host broadcasting in Los Angeles, the geniuses who ran the syndication business said that a female host could not succeed in national radio. The explanations ran the gamut from the grating nature of the female voice, to the belief that men would only listen to other men talking sports or politics.

Then, a Los Angeles advertiser who was selling boatloads of a product on my show decided that this so-called conventional wisdom was wrong, and we formed a partnership. As they say, the rest is radio history—not only was the show a success, it was a bigger success, and growing faster than any radio talk show in radio history.

So where were my "sisters" who should

DR. LAURA SCHLESSINGER is best known as "My Kid's Mom" on her internationally syndicated talk show, *Dr. Laura*. In it she "preaches, teaches, and nags" about morals, values, and ethics. She is heard by 20 million listeners each day and is the author of numerous books. Dr. Laura lives in California with her husband, Lewis, and their son, Deryk.

have been there to celebrate one small step for a woman, one large step for womankind? Did they put me on the cover of *Ms.* magazine? No. Did I get touted as Woman-of-the-Year? Nope. Not even when I was the first woman in the history of radio to win a Marconi, the industry's highest honor, for syndicated personality. Not a peep from NOW—the National Organization of I-don't-know-what-kind-of Women. No congratulatory calls from Gloria, Betty, or Pat Ireland. Of course, in all fairness to them, they may not have known about this break-through milestone for equality, because our "sisters" in the media saw to it that not a word of the award made it into print or onto TV news.

And I'm also another kind of should-be-feminist icon: I got a Ph.D. in Physiology from Columbia University in New York in the early 1970s. I was one of only three women to do so in another male-dominated venue. I also held full-time teaching positions in the Department of Biology at an East Coast college and at the University of Southern California, where I was the only female faculty member in the department. As for recognition of these accomplishments by the feminists, accomplishments based on hard work and sacrifice, in the immortal words of a well-known comedian, "I get no respect."

What's a girl gotta *do* to be a feminist role model?

Here I stand, having it all, and not getting a lick of credit for it from the feminist establishment. But then, I'm not a never-wed mother by choice; my child doesn't have a full-time nanny or a day-care to call "home"; I haven't divorced my husband and moved three thousand miles, graciously giving Dad e-mail visitation rights; I believe in adoption over abortion; I believe that marriage is a sacrament between a man and a woman; and I don't see masculine flattery as harassment. Yikes! I've answered my own question, haven't I?

And this was a movement I once embraced! Yes, friends, it's true, I am a "recovered" feminist. I must admit that during my college years, in the turbulent sixties, I embraced the notions of gender equality and liberation from stereotyped roles. I was enlightened—I had "the boots made for walkin'" and "I was woman, watch me roar." The point is, the once valiant women's movement that I embraced is no longer about fairness, equality, opportunity, and respect for *all* women—it's about the politics of selective diversity and, ultimately, of divisiveness. It is anti-female, anti-family, and anti-children. This is the real reason that I am not only *not* honored by the NOW, but, in fact, targeted by them for professional assassination.

Let me give you an example. In a 1997 syndicated newspaper column, a father wrote to ask me if he should pay for his daughter's second abortion that he was morally opposed to. I answered that he shouldn't pay for it, and that he should suggest that his daughter give the baby up for adoption. Considering the angry letter I got from the Feminist Caucus of the American Humanist Association, you'd think I'd told him to shoot her!

"Your advice," they wrote, "is tyrannical, anti-woman, inexcusable, punitive and makes you a public menace. Our organization will be urging that newspapers drop your column—the sooner, the better!"

Whew! For one *opinion*—that giving life and a home to a child was preferable to killing it—I should be silenced and my career destroyed.

Yup, that reaction embraces diversity all right! Isn't it reasonable, tolerant, and open to dialogue? Oh puhlease!

The phenomenal growth and success of my radio program has not been an unmixed blessing. It has been accompanied by the equally phenomenal growth of personal and professional attacks. The attacks we understand... the growth?

Well, in thinking about this talk, I began to see that at least one reason for the success of my radio show—with women, at least—is that it reflects my own growth as a human being. And my growth as a baby-boomer parallels that of a lot of my generation—those women born into middle-class families for whom a college education was an imperative and feminist ideals were a given. As young women we bought the package. We didn't have to be our mothers. We didn't have to stay home and take care of kids. We could have our own careers. Heck, we didn't even have to get married. We could just get out there and enjoy sex like the guys.

I even had my tubes tied, to make sure there were no accidents. I remember when I was teaching at the University of Southern California, a bright, young, married graduate student came to me to tell me that she was pregnant, and I reflexively said, "Oh, I'm so sorry." I was shocked, and somewhat embarrassed, when she told me not to feel sorry; that she was *glad* she was pregnant and that she and her husband had actually *planned* it.

That was my mindset when I began my radio career. The sky was the limit, and I didn't want any attachments to hold me back. I even remember telling my gentleman friend that he'd better not ever try to insinuate himself between me and my career because my career would win, hands-down. That voice suited the smart, well-informed audience of my contemporaries. I was one of them.

> What's a girl gotta do to be a feminist role model? Here I stand, having it all, and not getting a lick of credit for it from the feminist establishment.

It was also the seventies, and the Feminist Movement had begun to fix their sights on monogamy and sexual exclusivity as the next big obstacles to freedom. Women's liberation met sexual liberation—and they liked each other a lot. It was the era of feelings over facts; of doing your own thing—if it hurt someone, that was *their* problem; of throwing the baby out with the bath water—literally.

By this time I had become an academic expert in human sexuality. I had also been licensed as a psychotherapist in marriage and family counseling—a specialty whose quaint name was a hold-over from the days when people actually married—usually just once—and still had a family they *cared* about keeping intact.

I was definitely an evolving child of my devolving era. I was also a card-carrying nonbeliever (I didn't even give religion

enough thought to become an atheist). This put morality
somewhere between moot and entirely circumstantial. My new
career focus kept pace with the changing times and my local
radio show grew in popularity. All was well, and noncontro-
versial, for a number of years. But as the seventies drew to a
close, the multicareers, the successes, and all that freedom not
to commit, not to settle down, not to sacrifice, not to value
intimacy began to wear thin. It all culminated for me, one
evening in the early eighties, watching a NOVA special on
PBS with the man in my life—Lew Bishop. Lew had been
wanting to marry me for quite a while, but knew better than
to nag the little liberated woman about such a patriarchal,
bourgeois notion.

The program was an amazing documentary about the conception and gestation of a human embryo. Through the miracle of micro-fiber optics, you could see the sperm go through
the cervix, into the uterus, and then meet the egg in the fal-
lopian tube. Then, you could watch the development of a
human being from multiple cells, to a distinctly human
embryo and then fetus. Now, mind you, I was a physiology
Ph.D. and taught college developmental biology, but the science paled in comparison to the emotion of watching that
baby being born into the loving arms of an ecstatic, married,
mom and dad.

My life changed forever. Within months I was married and
pregnant. And, like many in my generation who waited too
long, it was not easy. We females are born with all the eggs

we're ever gonna have; and at age thirty-
eight, they're old, and they haven't been
refrigerated.

When finally Deryk was born it was the
best part of my life. Soon after giving birth,
I went to a think-tank feminist get-togeth-
er. The room was filled with heavy hitters,
from Betty on down. They were, a la
Khrushchev, slamming their shoes on the
table, complaining and yelling about gender prejudice, child-
care, politics, and so forth. Terrified, I rose up and dared to say,
"With all due respect to the cumulative IQ in this room, I have
two master's degrees, a Ph.D. and post-doctoral certification—
but the single most rewarding and important development in
my life is that I've become a mother. I'm distressed that everything spoken today about women's satisfaction ignores that."

You'd think I had passed gas in close quarters. The room got
very silent and people looked around at each other. I slunk
back into my chair, looking for the nearest exit. After what
seemed an eternity, other women spoke up in a similar vein. It
was as though I had given them the opening to say it's normal,
natural, and entirely wonderful for a woman to be feminine,
married, and a proud, hands-on mommy—that being a
woman isn't *all* about anger and power wars.

At that point I was Deryk's mommy all day long, leaving at
9 P.M. to go to work at the radio station till 1 A.M. I shifted to
middays once Deryk was in school. I had metamorphosed from

> We females are born with all the eggs we're ever gonna have: and at age thirty-eight, they're old, and they haven't been refrigerated.

the liberated psychotherapist to "I am my kid's mom." The role I had been taught to despise and disdain had given my life purpose, direction, and meaning. I wanted everyone to know that. So, I became an advocate for motherhood in advance of the rest of my cohort, who were also beginning to tire of the daily grind and the emotional emptiness, prodded by the inevitable, unforgiving advance of age and the lost opportunity to change their minds. Anne Taylor Fleming writes so movingly of this dilemma in her book, *Motherhood Deferred.*

I was an early pioneer in turning my back on liberation because it was too much about liberating myself from the femininity, womanhood, and motherhood at the core of each of us—movements be damned. Earlier today I said that I have it all—emphasis on "have." But I got it all, sequentially, not simultaneously. I was delighted to be tied down to a man I loved and to our child—yet I sorely missed being on the radio, the intense personal interaction with callers and listeners about what matters in life.

We also missed my paycheck and made do with one car that my husband drove to work. I rode a bicycle with Deryk in the child seat. It was touch and go with the mortgage. During this time our house was badly damaged in a fire, and my husband almost died of Sudden Death Syndrome, but he survived and we persevered.

Back on the air, I talked about the joys and struggles of family life gladly and often. I gave all female listeners permission to question the party line, to follow their hearts and deeper instinct. And I supported them when they did so. I think the thing I am proudest about in these later years is my support for parents who manage to put their children first in their lives, ahead of financial gain or career advancement. Daily I hear on the phone and in faxes, e-mails, and letters that I am the *only* voice they hear who champions their cause, who celebrates their decision to have at least one parent home with the kids when the kids themselves are at home. These parents, when brought on the air, proudly proclaim, "I am my kid's mom/dad." Fascinating that Ted Koppel once wondered aloud on *Nightline* that if I say, "I am my kid's mom," I aim to be provocative. Imagine—proclaiming one's joy in parenting is seen as provocative.

> I think the thing I am proudest about in these later years is my support for parents who manage to put their children first in their lives, ahead of financial gain or career advancement.

I also hear from the mothers and fathers I scold—those who had children for the same reasons they buy an SUV or designer shoes. They have a child because it's chic now to have children. It is another form of competition, and these parents want to win more than they want to parent. These parents sign their children up for fancy day-care while still in their first trimester of pregnancy. These folks have an unwillingness to give up one damn thing to make that child first in their lives—to put him or her at the pinnacle of their priorities. We know this because they substitute money and indulgence for love, and endless enrichment classes for time alone with mom and dad. As I say in the title of my latest book, "Don't Have 'Em If You Won't Raise 'Em!"

Many of these parents do succumb to my nagging...eventually. Their faxes usually start with, "I used to hate you. I'd turn off the radio when you came on. Now I see it was because I was feeling so guilty about leaving my son in day-care every day for eight hours. I just couldn't listen. I thought you just didn't understand and that what you were saying was just not doable." Then, later, they'd write again...to thank me, to tell me how wonderful and aggravating, how rewarding and difficult, how uplifting and upsetting it is to be a stay-at-home mom/dad. And, they also tell me they get lots of grief for giving up that six-figure job from friends and family, including their own mothers!

But the tide is turning. Young women don't hate being female, so they don't identify with today's radical feminists. They don't reject their potential as wives and mothers. They don't hate men, nor do they believe they cannot achieve their full potential. A major reason for their attitude is that the women's movement did level the playing field quite a bit. Women outnumber men in college, graduate, and professional schools—and their salaries are virtually at par with men the same age, who put in the same hours and have the same experience.

Many of these young women grew up in two-career families, and they know first-hand what children sacrifice in that environment. Those that don't reject marriage altogether (because they fear repeating their parents' serial divorces and remarriages), don't want to subject their future children to the loneliness and stress they experienced. I hear from them too.

In addition to moving from women's liberation to womanhood fulfilled, I also embarked on a spiritual path midway through life—another trend noted by social scientists among baby boomers. I am the product of what I have termed an "inter-faithless" marriage: my father a Jew; my Italian war-bride mother a Roman Catholic. No religion was practiced in the home. My father's parents rejected my mother because she wasn't Jewish. It tore our family apart.

> The Jewish people were chosen by God to be a light unto nations, and I believe that my nationwide preaching, teaching, and nagging about traditional morals, values, and ethics honors that mission.

Just as the NOVA special on birth woke me out of my feminist coma, another PBS show on the holocaust reintroduced me to my religious heritage. Deryk and I happened on the program by accident, tuning in just as mothers and children were being gunned down into ditches. This was no docudrama; it was actual Nazi footage. Deryk was only five or six, and we were both horrified. He asked me why the soldiers were killing those people. I answered that the soldiers were evil. Then he said, "Who are the mommies and the children?" I answered, "They are our people. They're Jews." He asked, "What's a Jew?" And my heart skipped a beat. I answered, "I don't really know, but I'm going to find out."

Today, the three of us are Orthodox Jews, who joyfully attend our Shul every Saturday and keep a Kosher home and observe the Sabbath. The Kosher part is less joyful, because it means I can never have another cheeseburger. But, it's a very small price to pay for the sense of belonging I feel having returned to my historical and spiritual roots.

Understanding Judaism has also given me a much deeper understanding of myself. The Jewish people were chosen by G-d* to be a "light unto the nations," and I believe that my nationwide preaching, teaching, and nagging about traditional morals, values, and ethics honors that mission. Now I know why I feel so committed to it.

Those tenacious naysayers—the Greek chorus that loves to follow my career and tell me what I can't do—chimed in again when I began to share my enthusiasm about discovering religion. They already saw my success as a woman in talk radio as some kind of fluke, but they were absolutely sure that if I kept talking about religion—especially about being a "Jew"—that my audience would abandon me in droves.

Once again, the so-called conventional wisdom was wrong. Once again, my timing, though accidental, was inspired. Millions of other people of my generation also began to ask that time-honored question, immortalized in song, "Is this all there is?" and finding, to their great relief, that the answer was,

* In the Orthodox Jewish tradition, the word God is not written out as a sign of respect.

"NO!" So, far from dooming my radio program, my religious conversation invigorated it, in addition to providing divine authority for my position on morality. Nor did the much-anticipated anti-Semitism ever rear its ugly head. As a matter of fact, Christian ministers and lay people openly endorsed me, writing me directly, writing books about me, and preaching about my show from their pulpits.

Needless to say, this latest turn in the road of my own personal journey endeared me...*not at all*...to the tattered-but-still-ferocious remnants of the once noble feminist movement. In the first place, it put us at loggerheads on the issue of abortion, and, since traditional morality is...ahem...a patriarchal conspiracy, my insistence on marriage as a condition for cohabitation and childbearing was a veritable declaration of war.

Now, there are a lot of things I could say about feminism's disastrous detour from the honorable goal of equal opportunity for women, but I would like to focus, in conclusion, on the most dangerous—the systematic eroding of the moral foundation of our society in the name of *freedom*. Today's feminists have joined their cause to that of pedophiles and perverts, who seek to destroy all sexual taboos in their *obsessive* quest to satiate their own sexual appetites under the guise of freedom. This unholy alliance is nowhere more visible than on our college campuses where:

- Sado-masochism clubs are as welcome as the Shakespeare Society (SUNY)
- Campus festivals celebrating free love, homosexual sex, transsexuality, and transvestitism are paid for by taxpayers

(Penn State)

■ Students are getting class credit for watching hard-core pornography and creating porn projects in—give me a break—Women's Studies Programs.

This is why I have come full circle from embracing feminism as a young woman to seeing it as Public Enemy Number One and saying so as loudly and as often as I can. While most young women don't identify as feminists today, too many of them have bought into the distorted view of licentiousness as freedom. Casual sex, experimentation with homosexuality and bisexuality, and abortion as birth control are seen by too many young people as *rights*. What no one tells them is that these behaviors also entitle them to a lifetime of emptiness, regret, and confusion, the probability of infertility, the loss of intimacy, and exposure to a whole host of acute and chronic diseases.

I deeply disdain the feminists for what they have done to generations of women and to children who pay the price of lost, intact, loving, stable homes with married committed moms and dads. I'm not shy about making my feelings known. I guess it's no surprise that despite my rise to the top of a male-dominated profession, I'm not likely to be the feminist poster girl any time soon.

But I cherish the fact that I *am* a hero to women and men of all ages who, like you, continue to revere our God-given roles and responsibilities, and I will continue to champion their contributions and sacrifices and be their proud spokesperson.

Thank you for inviting me to speak to you today when so

many groups are hostile or fearful. Thank you for all you do to make this a better world for *today's* children. ■

THE ENERGY, ADVEN-
TUROUSNESS, STO-
ICISM, AND COM-
PETITIVENESS OF NORMAL,
DECENT MALES ARE RESPONSI-
BLE FOR MUCH OF WHAT IS
RIGHT IN THE WORLD. ALL
AGES HAVE UNDERSTOOD THIS.
ALL HEALTHY SOCIETIES
APPRECIATE AND PRIZE THEIR
YOUNG MEN. WHY, IN THIS DAY
AND AGE, SHOULD WE BE
TURNING AGAINST THEM?
—CHRISTINA HOFF SOMMERS

THE WAR AGAINST BOYS

BY CHRISTINA HOFF SOMMERS
WASHINGTON, D.C., JANUARY 8, 1999
EXCERPTS FROM A SPEECH AT THE CONSERVATIVE WOMEN'S NETWORK

THERE IS A SURPRISING AMOUNT of hostility towards boys in this country. To put it bluntly: boys are politically incorrect. We may be the first society in history to turn against its male children.

I begin by describing a debate I had with celebrity lawyer, Gloria Allred, from California. Allred represented a fourteen-year-old girl who sued the Boy Scouts of America for excluding girls. She referred to same-sex scouting as a form of gender discrimination—she called it "gender apartheid."

I defended the Boy Scouts. I told her that younger boys and girls have different preferences and behaviors, citing the following homespun example. Hasbro Toys, a major toy manufacturing company, tested a playhouse the company was considering marketing to both boys and girls. But it soon emerged that girls and boys did not interact with the structure

in the same way. The girls dressed the dolls, kissed them, and played house. The boys catapulted the toy baby carriage from the roof. A Hasbro general

---

CHRISTINA HOFF SOMMERS is a resident scholar at the American Enterprise Institute. The author of *Who Stole Feminism? How Women Have Betrayed Women* and *The War Against Boys*, she has appeared on numerous television and radio shows. A mother of two sons, she and her husband live in Maryland.

manager came up with an explanation: boys and girls are different.

Allred flatly denied there are any innate differences. She seemed shocked by the boys' behavior. Apparently, she took it as a sign of potential violence. She said, "If there are some boys who catapult baby carriages off the roofs of doll houses, that is just an argument why we need to socialize [to train] boys at an earlier age, perhaps, to be playing with dolls."

Ms. Allred has powerful allies among educators. Gloria Steinem once said, "We need to raise boys more like we raise girls." Many schools are now following her advice, not because they don't like boys—and not because they want to harm males—but because they sincerely believe that something is seriously wrong with young men in America. A growing number of experts now claim that, as a group, the nation's boys are disturbed, depressed, and not in touch with their feelings and are therefore prone to violence. According to these critics, their masculinity, their idea of what it is to be male, is making them miserable and dangerous. Two psychologists at Harvard University, Carol Gilligan and William Pollack, have declared a national boy crisis. At the same time, hard-line feminists are persuaded that unless we intervene to change boys at the earliest possible age, women and girls will continue to be "oppressed under patriarchy." So there is a growing movement to save the males by making them less masculine.

Do American boys need to be saved? Do they need to be rescued from their masculinity? I do not think so. I do not agree that the nation's boys are in crisis. I see no evidence for it. Some boys, of course, are in serious trouble. So too are some girls. A small percentage of boys are antisocial and violent. But when looking at genuine social science research, you find that the vast majority of boys are mentally healthy. Being a boy is not a defect. It is not a disorder. It is not something you need to recover from.

The best way to explain the Save-the-Males movement is to describe some of the programs advocated by its founding members. Some of these descriptions may sound extreme. They are. But what worries me is that if no one stands up and protests, this thinking could easily become mainstream.

Take, for instance, the proposal by the Ms. Foundation for Women to create a national holiday for boys called "Sons Day." The Ms. Foundation, of course, created the school holiday for girls called Take Our Daughters to Work Day. But, to their consternation, many companies changed the day to Take Your Child to Work Day so as not to exclude boys. So the Ms. Foundation came up with the idea to design a separate holiday for boys called "Sons Day." Sounds great, right? Wrong. Here are some ways Sons Day was to be celebrated:

- Take your son for the day to an event that focuses on ending men's violence against women. Call 1-800 END ABUSE for more information.

- Plan a game or sport in which the contest does not keep score or declare a winner.

- Since Sons Day is on Sunday, get your son involved in

preparing the family for the work and school week ahead by helping lay out clothes for siblings and making lunches.

And for boys not totally exhausted by all the fun and excitement of the day's activities, the Ms. planners had a suggestion for the evening: Take your son grocery shopping then help him plan and prepare the family's evening meal.

As the Ms. staff had planned it, Sons Day wouldn't even give boys a day off from school. One friend of mine called it "a holiday in hell for Junior." In the end, Sons Day was cancelled and the Ms. Foundation has gone back to the drawing board trying to come up with a new plan to protect Take Our Daughters to Work Day. Nevertheless, their attempt to initiate a boy's holiday tells us something about how these reformers see boys. Clearly they regard boys as undomesticated, too competitive, and in serious need of reeducation.

Another example of the Save-the-Males movement is a new antisexual harassment guide funded by the U.S. Department of Education and distributed by the National Education Association called "Quit it!" Written by several women's groups, "Quit it!" is directed at the supposedly sexually harassing behavior of small children, especially boys, in kindergarten through third grade.

In the preface the authors explain that boys need special training, not necessarily because they are "bad" but because "we must all do a better job of addressing the aggressive behavior of young boys." So "Quit it!" introduces teachers to activities designed to calm boys down and make them less volatile.

One such recommended activity is a new, nonviolent, nonthreatening version of the game of tag. Here is what the guide advises teachers to do (p. 86):

> Before going outside to play, talk about how students feel when playing a game of tag. Do they like to be chased? Do they like to do the chasing? How does it feel to be tagged out? Get their ideas about other ways the game might be played.

It soon emerged that girls and boys did not interact with the playhouse structure in the same way. The girls dressed the dolls, kissed them, and played house. The boys catapulted the toy baby carriage from the roof.

After students share their fears and apprehensions about tag, the teacher is advised to announce that there is a new, nonthreatening version of the game called "Circle of Friends"—"where nobody is ever 'out'."

Perhaps some of the students experienced anger during playtime. The guide provides the teacher with the tools for organizing an in-class anger management workshop with the children. Reading it, you have to remind yourself that its suggestions are intended not for disturbed children but for normal five-to-seven-year-olds.

Here is how the *Boston Globe* describes one gender-fair school in Lexington, Massachusetts:

> Four years after it created its gender equity committee, Fiske Elementary is rife with signs of raised gender awareness. A quilt of

famous women, sewn by fifth-grade boys and girls, is displayed in the front hall. A wood sign on principal Joanne Benton's door declares this to be the "Princessipal's Office." Benton proudly maintains that "we have no single-sex table in our lunch room, and at recess, boys and girls play kickball together."

In more and more schools, boys are out of favor. Carol Kennedy, a longtime teacher and now principal of a school in Missouri, complacently told *The Washington Post*, "We do take away a lot of the opportunity to do things boys like to do. That is get rowdy, jump around. We don't allow that." Recess—the one time during the school day that boys can legitimately engage in rowdy play—is now under siege and may soon be a thing of the past.

In an extreme situation, about a month ago, four kindergarten boys in Sayreville, New Jersey, were suspended for three days for using their fingers as guns in a game of cops and robbers.

Why is all this happening now? Why would a leading women's group come up with a holiday for boys that involves calling 1-800 END ABUSE for suggested activities? Why is the Department of Education funding programs like "Quit it!" that treat young boys like fragile mental patients? As I said, there is deep concern that something is deeply wrong with boys. But what is it exactly? What is the problem with boys that justifies these extreme solutions?

In their defense, the Save-the-Males reformers point to the

high level of violence in American society. Most of it is perpetrated by males and a lot of it is directed against women. The reformers say they are trying to attack the problem at its root, to reach boys at the earliest possible age and redirect them

So there is a growing movement to save the males by making them less masculine.

away from aggression and violence and toward nurture and compassion. And they come armed with some alarming statistics that make their cause seem justified.

For example, Congress has created and the federal Department of Education supports an organization called the Womens Educational Equity Act Resource Center WEEA for short. On the WEEA website, a government supported website, mind you, there are some shocking statistics about male violence in American society. According to WEEA:

■ Violence is the leading cause of death for women.

■ Every year nearly 4 million women are beaten to death.

According to Katherine Hanson, the director of WEEA, these statistics are proof that males in our society are brought up to be aggressive, powerful, unemotional, and controlling. By her reckoning, the solutions proposed by programs like "Quit it!" and Sons Day to change the violent natures of boys make sense.

But there is just one problem. The statistics on this government-subsidized website are wildly false. They are, in fact, the most egregiously false statistics I think I have ever encountered.

Let's consider them in order of their shock value. First, the claim that 4 million American women are beaten to death each year by men.

Think about it. If the WEEA numbers are right, the United States is experiencing a level of carnage unparalleled in our century. Four million women beaten to death by men! Every year! That's 11,000 women a day!

In fact, the total number of annual female deaths in the entire country from all causes combined is approximately one million. Only a minuscule fraction of these deaths is caused by violence and an even tinier fraction is caused by battery. According to the FBI, the number of women who died from murder in 1996 was 3,631.

And the assertion that violence is the leading cause of death for women is equally false. For the record, the leading cause of death for women is heart disease, followed by cancer. But you wouldn't know it from visiting the WEEA website.

Ms. Hanson is deeply confused. There are women like her inside the Department of Education, in all the major women's advocacy groups, and at the Wellesley Center. Armed with egregiously false information, they believe passionately in the need to resocialize boys. She has suggested that one of the places to begin is Little League. Little League, says Hanson, "encourages aggressive, violent behavior."

The movement to Save-the-Males is predicated on what can be called a "women are from Venus, men are from hell" philosophy. This is the philosophy behind attacks on Little

League, and programs like "Quit it!" It informs the thought of the Princessipal in Lexington, Massachusetts, and administrators in New Jersey who suspended the kindergartners. It is the philosophy behind Sons Day.

> About a month ago, four kindergarten boys in Sayreville, New Jersey, were suspended for three days for using their fingers as guns in a game of cops and robbers.

It is absolutely true that males commit most of violent crime, at least 90 percent. But it is also true that the vast majority of males are not violent. In fact, according to the FBI, in any given year fewer than one percent of boys under eighteen are arrested for violent crimes.

It is not my position that boys need no improvement. All children need to be brought up with clear, distinct rules. But even more than little girls, little boys need structure and clear lines of authority. Boys who are ethically neglected have some very unpleasant ways of getting themselves noticed. It's not that girls are more moral than boys, they are not. Girls can be just as cruel and malicious as boys, if not more so. But cross-cultural studies have confirmed the obvious: boys are more physically aggressive.

In a classic 1973 study of male-female differences, Eleanor Maccoby and Carol Jacklin conclude that, compared to girls, boys engage in more mock fighting and more aggressive fantasies. They insult and hit one another, and retaliate more quickly when attacked.

These sex differences are found in very young children, as

soon as social play begins. A 1997 University of Vermont study compared parents' reports of children's behavior in twelve countries. Parents in the United States, Thailand, Greece, Jamaica, Puerto Rico, and Sweden reported that in every case, boys were more likely than girls to fight, swear, steal, throw tantrums, and threaten others.

Gloria Allred, Gloria Steinem, the authors of Sons Day, and many experts at Harvard and the Department of Education see these hitting, chasing, fighting, swearing, competitive creatures as future criminals. I just see boys.

I think it was the social theorist Hannah Arendt who said that every year civilization is invaded by millions of tiny barbarians—they're called children. Every society confronts the problem of civilizing its children, particularly its young males. History teaches that masculinity constrained by morality is powerful and constructive; it also teaches that masculinity without morality is terribly destructive.

We have a set of proven social practices for raising young men. The traditional approach is through character education: to develop a young man's sense of honor and help him become a considerate, conscientious human being. In short, to turn him into a gentleman. This approach respects boys' masculine natures. It is time-tested and it works. Even today, despite several decades of moral confusion, most young men understand the term "gentleman" and approve of the ideals it connotes.

What the save-the-males reformers are proposing is quite

different. They seek to civilize boys by res-
cuing them from their masculinity. "Raise
boys more like we raise girls," is Gloria
Steinem's advice. This approach is deeply
disrespectful of boys.

I have been critical of some feminists in
my talk today, but I'd like to end on an
optimistic note. The subtitle of my book
The War Against Boys is "how misguided
feminism is harming our young men."
But there is a more generous and accepting kind of feminism that I strongly
believe in—a feminism that asserts equality between men and women but also
accepts their differences. A feminism that
calls for fairness and understanding for both males and
females.

> The energy, adventur-
> ousness, stoicism, and
> competitiveness of nor-
> mal, decent males are
> responsible for much
> of what is right in the
> world. All ages have
> understood this. All
> healthy societies
> appreciate and prize
> their young men. Why,
> in this day and age,
> should we be turning
> against them?

Last year a book came out called *Between Mothers and Sons*. It
is a collection of stories by feminist writers about what it is
like to have a son. When I first saw it I thought it would be
full of stories of mothers trying to save their sons from the violence and militaristic hegemony of the patriarchy. I expected
to feel sorry for the boys. But the book surprised me. It turned
out to be full of stories of women rediscovering the nature of
boys, accepting it, and ultimately delighting in it.

Deborah Gaylen, a short story writer and essayist, describes
what happened when she sent her son Dylan to a Montessori

preschool "run by a goddess-worshipping, multi-cultural women's collective on Cape Cod:"

> Something about it did not honor his boy soul. I think it was the absence of physical competition. Boys who clashed or tussled with each other were separated and counseled by the peacemakers. Sticks were confiscated and turned into tomato stakes in the school garden.

After agonizing over how she, a good feminist and a good pacifist, could be the mother of a stick-wielding, weapon-generating boy, Gaylen comes upon the answer. She writes:

> A five-year-old boy, I learned from reading summaries of various neurological studies, is a beautiful, fierce, testosterone drenched, cerebrally asymmetrical humanoid carefully engineered to move objects through space, or, at the very least, to watch others do so.

Janet Burroway, a poet, novelist, and self-described pacifist-liberal, has a son Tim who grew up to become a career soldier. She is not sure how exactly he came to move in a direction opposite her own. She recalls his abiding fascination with plastic planes, toy soldiers, and military history, noting that "his direction was early set."

Tim takes her aback in many ways, but she is clearly proud of him. Throughout his childhood she was struck by his "chivalric character." "He would," she writes, "literally lay down his life for a cause or a friend. I am forced to be aware of my own contradictions in his presence: a feminist often charmed by his machismo."

Gaylen and Burroway discard some common anti-male prejudices when they discover that boys have their own distinctive graces and virtues. The love and respect they share with their sons leads them to overcome the fashionable resentments that many females harbor toward males. My suggestion is that, as a society, we follow the example of these feminist mothers and rediscover the goodness of boys. We need to stop treating the Dylans and Tims and Boy Scouts and Little Leaguers of the world as if they are afflicted with a disorder called boyness.

It is unfashionable to say so, but I will say it anyway: The energy, adventurousness, stoicism, and competitiveness of normal, decent males are responsible for much of what is right in the world. All ages have understood this. All healthy societies appreciate and prize their young men. Why, in this day and age, should we be turning against them?

If you are an optimist, as I am, you believe that good sense and fair play will prevail. If you are a mother of sons, as I am, you know that one of the more agreeable facts of life is that boys will be boys. ■

WASHINGTON IS SPENDING MONEY AT A RATE OF $3 MILLION A MINUTE. AN AVERAGE FAMILY PAYS 40 PERCENT OF ITS INCOME IN TAXES—MORE THAN FOOD, CLOTHING, SHELTER, AND TRANSPORTATION COMBINED.

—VIRGINIA THOMAS

THE FEDERAL GOVERNMENT—
HUGE, WASTEFUL, AND
INEFFICIENT: *What Can We Do?*

BY VIRGINIA THOMAS
WASHINGTON, D.C., FEBRUARY 11, 2000
EXCERPTS FROM A SPEECH AT THE CONSERVATIVE WOMEN'S NETWORK

THE QUESTION BEFORE US today is this: "What can you and I do to preserve freedom for another generation and work against the tide of bigger, more centralized government that confiscates more of our money, oversees more of our lives, and controls more of our decisions and our property?"

Few people are aware of the scope of their government—of its overall size, of its spending on a day-to-day basis. Today, Washington responds to problems by automatically taking over, never asking if programs already exist for the same purpose, or if existing programs are working, or if there's a better option to solving the problem.

Remember how America was transfixed by the horror of the Columbine High School shooting? Washington's immediate

answer was to institute new programs; the Left sought to have greater gun controls; the Right wanted to post the Ten Commandments. And the House

VIRGINIA THOMAS is director of Executive Branch Relations at The Heritage Foundation. She was a top aide to House Majority Leader Richard Armey, a deputy assistant secretary of the U.S. Department of Labor (in the George H. W. Bush administration), and worked as labor counsel for the U.S. Chamber of Commerce.

passed a bill that would add at least six new programs on top of the 117 that already exist at the federal level to serve at-risk, or delinquent youth.

Now, these 117 programs are administered by fifteen different departments, and they cost taxpayers over $4.4 billion every year. And yet no one has bothered to ask if they are working. We don't know which tools of governance work most effectively—whether it's boot camps or incarceration, character education or mentoring, gang intervention or counseling, advertisements or grants—we just don't know. We only know that we care, so we send money, and spend money, and set up new programs.

Please bear with me as we do a reality check on government. Spending is out of control. It's unrestrained by the previous mantras that used to limit federal spending, such as "Let's not have deficit spending." The fact is we have a national debt of $5.6 trillion that drains 11 to 14 percent of our annual budget just in interest payments—that's $229 billion every year. Interest on the national debt is our third largest federal program.

The Republican Congress—I used to be a proud warrior of that revolution—has lost its focus, or at least those representatives and senators who were willing to cast their votes for smaller government and reduced spending. What I'm about to tell you is known to few people.

The percentage of congressional Republicans who voted to increase federal spending was 21 percent in the 104th

Congress, 1995-1996. In the 105th Congress, it was 33 percent. And last year—99 percent! The percentage of the Senate, according to the National Taxpayers Union, was 100 percent. The swiftness of the turnabout is breathtaking. No, we're not making progress on rolling back the welfare state.

In 1996 there were 417 House members whose votes, as an average, would have reduced federal spending, as well as ninety-five senators. But in 1999 there were only two House members, Jim Sensenbrenner and Ron Paul. No amendment to reduce spending by $1 billion or more has been passed since 1997. The last and largest spending cut vote attempted was offered by Congressman Tom Coburn, who unfortunately is leaving. It only got 101 votes: 97 Republicans and 4 Democrats.

For most of this nation's history until 1971 the entire federal government was funded by less than $200 billion every year. Today it costs $1.8 *trillion*. Washington is spending money at a rate of $3 million a minute. Our tax burden is at an all-time, peace-time high. An average family pays 40 percent of its income in taxes—more than food, clothing, shelter, and transportation combined. We pay more than $7,000 in taxes for every man, woman, and child in this country. And tax revenues have increased since Bill Clinton came to power in 1992 by $785 billion.

And the size of government? President Clinton and Vice President Gore told America in 1992 that our government is smaller than it was when John F. Kennedy was president. The truth is that we are living with a huge shadow government. It is a work force of at least 17 million people. These are contract employees, working within the federal government. And the numbers are growing.

The Agriculture Department will tell you that they had a 7 percent cut in the number of their civil servants, but they expanded their contract work force by 8 percent. The State Department showed a 5 percent cut, but had an increase in contract workers of 111 percent. The Education Department showed a 6 percent cut, but had a 129 percent increase in contract workers.

Five departments increased in size too, which you don't hear about—Commerce, Justice, Transportation, Treasury, and the Environmental Protection Agency. In 1995, the latest data available, the cost of the federal work force for direct payroll was $103 billion. The dollar value of federal service contracts with private companies was $114 billion. Obviously, then, you have almost as big a network outside the government, surrounding the government, as in the government itself.

Then there is waste. At least $350 billion in waste is documented each year. Last year, the GAO told Senator Fred Thompson that it had uncovered $19 billion in overpayments from the seven large federal social programs. Think of that money as down the drain, all $19 billion of it.

What could you buy for $19 billion? The entire HUD Section 8 program with a little left over. You could buy all the kindergarten through twelfth grade programs run by the

Department of Education. You could run the entire Veterans Hospital system. You could even have a tax cut, God forbid.

> Washington responds to problems by automatically taking over, never asking if there's a better option to solving the problem.

You can go through every department or agency and save billions by stopping the fraud, waste, duplication, and mismanagement. HUD, for example, gave $857 million in 1998 in rent subsidy payments erroneously.

Who's minding the store? Do you know that the federal government now owns more than a third of all the land in the United States? That is truly remarkable. I was interested to learn from the Senate Banking Committee that the Community Reinvestment Act—a very small program begun in 1997 to encourage banks to loan to disadvantaged communities—has credit allocations that top $1.05 trillion. (The bulk of that occurred under Bill Clinton.)

In 1998, Community Reinvestment Act commitments to disadvantaged groups was $694 billion—more than the gross domestic product of all Canada—and they don't tell what they do with this credit. This one small program started in 1977.

IRS administers a tax code of some 17,000 pages. Medicare regulations consist of 134,000 pages, which inhibit flexibility, threaten privacy, and challenge the integrity of doctors who do what they are educated to do.

A recent report on veterans hospitals showed that over a two-year period, three thousand medical errors resulted in seven hundred deaths. And then there's the gene therapy research. I'm always troubled when I don't see a Republican name, or *someone's* name, being outraged about patient safety, or federal funds being spent killing people, literally.

Who's minding the store? The performance numbers of the Legal Services Corporation collapsed right in front of them upon a record audit. They had boasted that they had served 1.9 million poor people, when in fact it was 1.1 million. And yet, Congress increased their budget by around $5 million.

Are we in fact a monarchy? Think about this.

The executive branch between April of 1996 and the end of September of 1999 issued a number of rules—in fact, 15,280 final rules. In that very same period, Congress—through compromises, negotiations, House subcommittees, Senate subcommittees, the whole legislative process—only passed 667 laws. And they all have the same force of law.

Paul Begala, who worked at the Clinton White House a couple of years ago, sounded like a teenager driving a car for the first time when he spoke about signing executive orders. He said, "Stroke of the pen, law of the land, kind of cool." A far distance from the founders, who knew that we had to restrain centralized government, and arbitrary petty government.

How about government dependency? Our passion against government's intrusiveness seems to dissipate when we start receiving favors or benefits from that entity.

Look around and you can see that political dependency is growing as fast as federal spending. At least 90 million

Americans are directly dependent on government handouts or jobs as contrasted to
the country's 82 million private employees.
James Bovard, who has written a great book,
Freedom in Chains, describes the millions of
people who get SSI, Social Security, welfare,
food stamps, federal subsidies of one sort or

We are living with a huge shadow govern-ment. It is a work force of at least 17 million people.

another, school lunches, Medicaid, housing, and on and on.

Government dictates. Some of the things the government is
telling us to do are so small that we cannot muster a sense of
outrage. The government dictates the number of pounds of
raisins that California farmers sell this year; the number of pairs
of Indonesian panties and bathrobes American consumers will
be permitted to buy; the number of acres of land Uncle Sam
pays farmers to leave idle; the types of garments, if any, women
may sew in their own homes.

So what can we do? What actions are possible? Let me
throw out a few thoughts.

There are two kinds of people: those who take from government, and those who give; those who fight against the government's growth, and those who don't. Is doing nothing an
option for you and me? I don't think so. I think we would
never abandon the field for the sake of our children, our grandchildren, the nephews and nieces who will one day look up at
us and say, "What did you do when you were there? Why am
I living with this? If you had done more, I wouldn't have this
government."

We must convert our vision into substance; we must learn some political skills.

We want to restore integrity and accountability to government. Here is one way. If any given program shows no evidence of effectiveness, why not terminate it? There's a 1993 law called "The Government Performance and Results Act" that a number of committees in the House and Senate have been working on in a very quiet way. It would use performance information to drive decisions. Should it be successful—if it continues, if it's credible, if it has integrity—it could change the culture of Washington. For example, a Sunset amendment that would eliminate ineffective programs that Congressman Bob Schaffer of Colorado offered to the Juvenile Justice Bill last year had a simple amendment that said something along the lines that, "If no existing programs can prove that they're effective in a certain amount of time, they would be sunset."

At first the people in power resisted it. But then you can't really resist it very credibly and very vocally. And so it ended up passing on the House floor in June 1999 with the backing of 210 Republicans and 153 Democrats. It could well serve as a model both for Washington and state governments.

New York City did it with its police department. Under Mayor Rudolf Guiliani they started managing by performance and results. They evaluated where, when, and how crimes occurred each day. They focused enforcement efforts and resources in critical areas. They evaluated the performance of individual precincts, and held precinct commanders personally accountable for the performance of the precinct. As a result homicides and felonies dropped to the lowest levels in twenty years.

This is simple common sense. You have to pick that part of the world where you have jurisdiction, whether on Capitol Hill or outside the Hill, and focus on performance, get objective answers, and then change the way Washington works and spends money.

Now, compared to the executive branch, Congress has incredibly low resources. I was astonished to learn that of the total federal work force, the legislative branch has only 1.1 percent, or about 30,000 people. Reduce that to the number of committee staff who are in a position to oversee all the rest of government and you come down to about 130 people—130 people in the House and the Senate who oversee the executive branch.

And their helpmates? We have the GAO, the inspectors general, and on the outside, such organizations as The Heritage Foundation or the Family Research Council, the Cato Institute or all of us. The question I ask is, What can we do on the outside to help make it easier for the people in power to make the right decisions?

Finally, I would like to suggest that we could all be a truth squad. We could all learn more about government, talk more about it.

In conclusion, as you can see, we really can't rely on the government to police itself, or the media to police government, or even Congress to police government. We must all pick up this wagon and help—help prevent such horrors as the Columbine shooting. We must realize that our culture today is bent on sapping religion, eschewing moral precepts. It has thrown out such virtues as self-restraint, self-discipline, and self-mortification, respect for authority, truth, honor, patience.

In their place we have a culture that promotes division and diversity and self-expression, even animalistic self-expression. Look at the media, look at Hollywood, which wallow in this narcissistic self-expression.

I would like to read you a "poem" that was given to ninth graders in an English class in a public school in Minerva, Ohio. The teacher asked the kids to replicate this format, this expression, these ideas, in a way that resonated in their own lives. It's called Revolutionary Spanish Lesson.

"Whenever my name was mispronounced, I want to buy a toy pistol, put on dark sunglasses, push my beret to an angle, comb my beard to a point, hijack a busload of Republican tourists from Wisconsin, force them to chant anti-American slogans in Spanish, and wait for the bilingual swat team to helicopter over head begging me to be reasonable."

Reading such trash we might feel overwhelmed—we have lost. But we haven't lost. We cannot lose, for our children's sake, and for the next generation's sake. ■

ABOUT THE CLARE BOOTHE LUCE POLICY INSTITUTE

THE CLARE BOOTHE LUCE POLICY INSTITUTE, a 501 (c) (3) non-profit Virginia corporation, was founded in 1993.

The Luce Policy Institute has a two-pronged mission: (1) to take conservative ideas to young women and to mentor them into effective leaders, and (2) to expand school choice opportunities for children in kindergarten through twelfth grade.

By promoting outstanding women leaders who advocate lower taxes, a strong national defense, free enterprise, limited government, and strong families, the Luce Policy Institute provides support for women who want a good marriage, a family, and a career. We highlight role models for women at home and at work, with Clare Boothe Luce herself serving as an example.

A variety of programs are offered to young women and others eager to learn about conservative ideas.

The audience listens intently to a Conservative Women's Network luncheon speaker.

LEADERSHIP TRAINING

In Washington, D.C., and on college campuses, the Luce Policy Institute assembles young women for hands-on training in fighting for conservative principles and refuting radical feminist propaganda. Leadership instructors have included national talk radio host Janet Parshall, former welfare mother turned welfare reform activist Star Parker, former U.S. Treasurer Bay Buchanan, pro-life activist Carmen Pate, Miss District of Columbia 2000 Rashida Jolley, and many others who give of themselves to mentor young women.

The staff, board, and close advisors are constantly involved in teaching America's most promising young women. In addition to mentoring luncheons, the Luce Policy Institute offers internships for young women. These highly coveted slots give a tremendous boost to young women.

Rashida Jolley, (right) Miss District of Columbia, 2000, talks to young women at a high school mentoring luncheon.

Clare Boothe Luce Policy Institute 2001 Summer interns pose with Linda Chavez at Conservative Women's Network Luncheon. From left, Jill Novotny, Linda Chavez, Kellie Smith, and Andrea Schnell.

TOPICAL CONFERENCES

The Luce Policy Institute holds conferences around the nation on issues of critical importance. The Institute, for example, held a conference in California on the topic of affirmative action when feminists were seeking to foster dependency based programs upon special preferences.

CONSERVATIVE WOMEN SPEAKERS PROGRAM

Each semester, the Luce Policy Institute sponsors top conservative women to lecture at schools around the nation. Many of these prominent women are featured in this book. These conservative speakers include Ann Coulter, Bay Buchanan, Christina Hoff Sommers, Suzanne Fields, Michelle Easton, Carmen Pate, Star Parker, and many others. These lecturers are often the only conservative women students will be exposed to in their four years of college. At one highly effective campus lec-

Luce speaker Ann Coulter talks with students at Wittenberg University following her campus lecture on the war on terrorism.

ture at Wittenberg University in Ohio, columnist Ann Coulter addressed more than three hundred college students on the war on terrorism, and subsequently spoke individually to many of the young men and women. Extensive interaction between speakers and students is typical of Luce Policy Institute events.

RADICAL FEMINIST EXPOSE

The Institute tracks feminists' activities and policy on gender sensitivity training, among other issues, in grade schools and Women's Studies courses on college campuses. We publish the truth about the feminists for students, parents, and the media. Many of our nationally published articles have been featured on the Rush Limbaugh Show, the Dr. Laura Show, and a slew of other talk radio programs.

EDUCATION

The Luce Policy Institute seeks to expand school choice opportunities for children in kindergarten through twelfth grade. The Institute also honors the dedicated parents and education activists who invest their love, lives, and livelihoods into training the minds and hearts of children. Through writing, research, conferences, and grassroots policy work the Institute promotes school choice and academically rigorous schools. Focusing always on the child.

A student at Luce Policy Institute's 2001 Annual Capitol Hill Seminar in Rayburn House Office Building asks a question of a speaker.

The Institute's quarterly newsletter educates readers on conservative principles.

PUBLICATIONS

The Luce Policy Institute publishes up-to-date quarterly newsletters, policy issue papers, and opinion pieces in national newspapers to help educate and motivate mainstream Americans who are tired of radical feminist nonsense and long to hear a voice of reason on issues such as sexual harassment in elementary schools, free speech on college campuses, and leftist Women's Studies courses.

WWW.CBLPOLICYINSTITUTE.ORG

Archived on the Luce website are issue and policy papers, speeches and articles on a wide range of subjects, including school choice, Women's Studies departments, coed military training, Title IX, Social Security privatization, and radical feminism. And more information on the Luce Institute's programs, as well as the Conservative Women's Studies Bookstore—a list of books from the prominent and insightful conservative women that college and university Women's Studies departments omit from their curriculums. ■

Luce Policy Institute
President Michelle Easton
speaks to students at a
Luce Policy Institute
Conference in 1999,
Grand Rapids, Michigan,
titled "Freedom, Faith and
Family... One Generation
Away from Extinction."

Give the Gift of

GREAT
AMERICAN
Conservative
WOMEN

❦

To friends, colleagues, or as a high school
or college graduation gift for young women.

❦

❑ YES, please send me _____ copies of *Great American Conservative Women* for $18.00 each.

PLEASE CHARGE MY:

❑ VISA   ❑ MasterCard   ❑ [American Express]   ❑ DISCOVER NOVUS

NAME _____

ORGANIZATION _____

ADDRESS _____

CITY/STATE/ZIP _____

PHONE _____

EMAIL _____

CARD NO. _____

EXPIRATION DATE _____

SIGNATURE _____

Call 1-888-891-4288
E-MAIL US AT CBLPI@EROLS.COM
FAX: 703-318-8867

Please include $3.00 shipping and handling for one book and an
additional $1.50 for each additional book. Allow 3 weeks for delivery.

Make check or money order payable to:
Clare Boothe Luce Policy Institute and return to:

Clare Boothe Luce Policy Institute
Attn: Book Orders
112 Elden Street, Suite P • Herndon, Virginia 20170